Betty Crocker

christmas
cookies

100 Delicious Recipes

WILEY

Wiley Publishing, Inc.

Copyright © 2010 by General Mills, Minneapolis, Minnesota. All rights reserved.

Published by Wiley Publishing, Inc., Hoboken, New Jersey

For general information on our other products and services or for technical support, please contact our Customer Care Department within the United States at (877) 762-2974, outside the United States at (317) 572-3993 or fax (317) 572-4002.

Wiley also publishes its books in a variety of electronic formats. Some content that appears in print may not be available in electronic books. For more information about Wiley products, visit our web site at www.wiley.com.

Library of Congress Cataloging-in-Publication Data:
Betty Crocker christmas cookies : 100 delicious recipes.
   p. cm.
  Includes index.
  ISBN 978-1-4351-2573-5 (cloth)
  1. Cookies. 2. Christmas cookery. I. Crocker, Betty. II. Title:
Christmas cookies.
  TX772.B54 2010
  641.5'686—dc22

2010013136

General Mills

Editorial Director:
Jeff Nowak

Publishing Manager:
Christine Gray

Editor:
Grace Wells

Recipe Development and Testing:
Betty Crocker Kitchens

Photography: General Mills Photography Studios and Image Library

Wiley Publishing, Inc.

Publisher: Natalie Chapman

Associate Publisher: Jessica Goodman

Executive Editor: Anne Ficklen

Editor: Meaghan McDonnell

Production Manager: Michael Olivo

Production Editor: Abby Saul

Cover Design: Suzanne Sunwoo

Art Director: Tai Blanche

Layout: Indianapolis Composition Services

Manufacturing Manager: Tom Hyland

Printed in China
10 9 8 7 6 5 4 3 2 1

Cover photo: Gingerbread Cookies (page 86) and Espresso Thumbprint Cookies (page 88)

Our Betty Crocker Kitchens seal guarantees success in your kitchen. Every recipe has been tested in America's Most Trusted Kitchens™ to meet our high standards of reliability, easy preparation and great taste.

Find more great ideas at *BettyCrocker*.com

Dear Friends,

What better way to spread cheer than with Christmas cookies? When the holidays roll around, this great collection of recipes will help you celebrate all season long.

There's no busier time than Christmas so whenever you are pressed for time, turn to the chapter on Easy Cookies and Bars. Favorites like Mary's Chocolate Chip Cookies and Oatmeal Raisin Cookies will be ready in no time! If you're looking for recipes that are sure to be crowd-pleasers, try baking classics like Hazelnut Biscotti and Russian Tea Cakes.

There's nothing merrier than filling your home with festive treats like Christmas Cookie Packages and Peppermint Swirls. Even kids can join in the fun by helping to decorate Gingerbread Cookies and Jolly Santa Cookies. And don't forget to share your freshly baked goodies! Family and friends will be delighted with a gift of delicious cookies or other home-baked treats like Deluxe Christmas Fudge and Luscious Chocolate Truffles.

Once the wonderful aroma of freshly baked Christmas cookies fills your home, you won't want the holidays to end!

Warmly,

Betty Crocker

contents

Holiday Baking Secrets

Cookie Baking Tips

- Have at least three or four cookie sheets on hand so that as you bake one sheet you can get another one ready to go. Use cookie sheets that are at least 2 inches narrower and shorter than the inside dimensions of your oven so heat circulates around them.

- We recommend baking only one cookie sheet at a time, using the middle oven rack. If you want to bake two sheets at the same time, put one on the oven rack in the upper third of the oven and one on the oven rack in the lower third. Remember to switch their positions halfway through baking time.

- Check cookies at the minimum bake time. Even 1 minute can make a difference with cookies, especially those high in sugar and fat. The longer cookies bake, the more brown, crisp or hard they become.

- Always put cookie dough on completely cooled cookie sheets. Cookies spread too much if put on a hot, or even warm, cookie sheet. You can cool cookie sheets quickly by popping them in the refrigerator or freezer or by running cold water over them (dry completely and grease again if needed).

Storing Christmas Treats

Here's a great tip to remember: Store crisp cookies with other crisp ones; soft cookies with other soft ones; chewy cookies with other chewy ones. Never store crisp and chewy or soft cookies together in the same container or the crisp cookies will become soft.

- Store crisp cookies at room temperature in a loosely covered container.

- Store chewy and soft cookies at room temperature in resealable food-storage plastic bags or a tightly-covered container.

- Let frosted or decorated cookies set or harden before storing; store them between layers of waxed paper, plastic wrap or foil.

- Store different flavors of cookies in separate containers, or they'll pick up the flavors of the other cookies.

- Most bars can be stored tightly covered, but check the recipe to make sure. Some may need to be loosely covered, and others may need to be refrigerated.

- To freeze cookies and bars, tightly wrap and label; freeze unfrosted cookies up to 12 months and frosted cookies up to three months. Do not freeze meringue, custard-filled or cream-filled cookies. Put delicate frosted or decorated cookies in single layers in freezer containers, and cover with waxed paper before adding another layer; freeze. Thaw most cookies, covered, in the container at room temperature for one to two hours. For crisp cookies, remove from the container to thaw.

Host a Christmas Cookie Exchange!

Call it a Sweets Swap or a Cookie Exchange; you'll get to go home with the same great results—and lighten your baking load, too. Why not start this tradition of sharing with your friends this year? Here's how:

- Send out invitations a month in advance. Think about limiting your group to fewer than 12 people to make managing the event easier. You may want to mail labels for the sweets along with the invitations.

- Ask guests to bring their sweets on paper or plastic plates or in nonreturnable containers and cover them with clear plastic wrap so the goodies are easily seen. Each person needs to bring enough treats to share and sample.

- Everyone will want the recipes, so have guests bring a copy; e-mail the recipes or print them out. As host, you'll need to provide the space for guests and their treats. Be sure you have lots of piping-hot coffee and tea to go with the cookie samples.

Holiday Shortbread

Create your own shortbread masterpieces! Try the Shortbread Buttons, Ornaments or Trees, and your cookies will get oohs and aahs!

Shortbread

Prep Time: 45 min ▪ Start to Finish: 1 hr 15 min ▪ About 2 dozen cookies

> ³/₄ cup butter or margarine, softened
> ¹/₄ cup sugar
> 1³/₄ cups all-purpose flour
> ¹/₂ teaspoon almond extract, if desired

1 Heat oven to 350°F. In large bowl, beat butter and sugar with electric mixer on medium speed, or mix with spoon. Stir in flour and almond extract. (If dough is crumbly, mix in additional 1 to 2 tablespoons butter or margarine, softened.)

2 On lightly floured surface, roll dough into 9 × 6-inch rectangle, ½ inch thick. Cut into 1½-inch squares with knife or cut with 1½-inch cookie cutters. On ungreased cookie sheet, place squares or shapes about 1 inch apart.

3 Bake 12 to 14 minutes or until set. Remove from cookie sheet to cooling rack. Cool completely, about 30 minutes.

1 Cookie: Calories 90 (Calories from Fat 50); Total Fat 6g (Saturated Fat 3g); Cholesterol 15mg; Sodium 40mg; Total Carbohydrate 9g (Dietary Fiber 0g); Protein 1g

If you like pastel colors for cookie dough, tint using liquid food colors. For brightly colored doughs, you'll get the best results with paste food colors. Paste food color is available in craft and specialty kitchen stores. To color the doughs for Shortbread Buttons, Shortbread Ornaments and Shortbread Trees, we used paste food colors, kneading the color into the dough in a 1-quart food storage plastic resealable bag. This is an activity kids love!

Shortbread Buttons: Tint cookie dough with food color. Roll dough ¼ inch thick; cut with 1½-inch round cookie cutter. Make button holes with toothpick or end of straw; bake as directed. About 3 dozen cookies.

Shortbread Ornaments: Divide dough into 3 equal parts. Tint each part with food colors to make bright red, green and purple. Roll dough between sheets of waxed paper to ¼-inch thickness; cut with 3-inch round biscuit cutter. Cut dough rounds with knife or pizza cutter to form ¼-inch strips. Combine different colors of dough strips to form striped round ornaments. Pinch small pea-size amount of dough; place on ornament to form top. Punch hole near top with end of plastic straw to hang ornament; bake as directed. Decorate with decorating gels if desired. About 2 dozen cookies.

Shortbread Trees: Divide dough into 6 equal parts. Mix 2 parts dough, 2 tablespoons chopped pistachio nuts and enough green food color to tint dough a light green. Mix another 2 parts dough and enough green food color to tint dough a medium green. Mix remaining 2 parts dough and enough green food color to tint dough a deep green. Pat light green dough into 9 × 2-inch rectangle, ¾ inch thick, on plastic wrap. Pat medium green dough into 9 × 1¾-inch rectangle, ½ inch thick; place on top of light green dough. Pat deep green dough into 9 × ¾-inch roll, ½ inch thick; place on top of medium green dough. Shape dough into triangle so it looks like a tree shape (don't worry if layers aren't perfect). Wrap dough in plastic wrap and refrigerate about 2 hours or until firm. Cut dough into ¼-inch slices. Place about 1 inch apart on ungreased cookie sheet. Bake 10 to 12 minutes or until set. Cool on cookie sheet 1 minute before removing to cooling rack. About 2 dozen cookies.

1

easy cookies and bars

Mary's Chocolate Chip Cookies

Prep Time: 1 hr ■ Start to Finish: 1 hr ■ About 3¹/₂ dozen cookies

1¹/₂ cups butter or margarine, softened
1¹/₄ cups granulated sugar
1¹/₄ cups packed brown sugar
1 tablespoon vanilla
2 eggs
4 cups all-purpose flour
2 teaspoons baking soda
¹/₂ teaspoon salt
1 bag (24 oz) semisweet chocolate chips (4 cups)

1 Heat oven to 375°F. In large bowl, mix butter, sugars, vanilla and eggs with spoon. Stir in flour, baking soda and salt (dough will be stiff). Stir in chocolate chips.

2 Onto ungreased cookie sheet, drop dough by level ¼ cupfuls about 2 inches apart. Flatten slightly with fork.

3 Bake 12 to 15 minutes or until light brown (centers will be soft). Cool slightly. Remove from cookie sheet to cooling rack; cool.

1 Cookie: Calories 245 (Calories from Fat 110); Total Fat 12g (Saturated Fat 7g); Cholesterol 30mg; Sodium 140mg; Total Carbohydrate 32g (Dietary Fiber 1g); Protein 2g

Chocolate chip cookies date back to 1940 when Ruth Wakefield of The Toll House Inn of Massachusetts chopped a bar of leftover semisweet chocolate and added it to a basic cookie recipe. Later that day, Toll House Cookies made the news when a visiting writer got a taste of the new cookie. That same year, chocolate chip cookies were introduced to homemakers on the Betty Crocker coast-to-coast radio series, *Famous Foods from Famous Places*.

White Chocolate Chunk– Macadamia Cookies

Prep Time: 1 hr ■ Start to Finish: 1 hr ■ About 2½ dozen cookies

1 cup packed brown sugar
½ cup granulated sugar
½ cup butter or margarine, softened
½ cup shortening
1 teaspoon vanilla
1 egg
2¼ cups all-purpose flour
1 teaspoon baking soda
¼ teaspoon salt
1 package (6 oz) white chocolate baking bars, cut into ¼- to ½-inch chunks
1 jar (3.25 oz) macadamia nuts, coarsely chopped

1 Heat oven to 350°F. In large bowl, beat sugars, butter, shortening, vanilla and egg with electric mixer on medium speed until light and fluffy, or mix with spoon. Stir in flour, baking soda and salt (dough will be stiff). Stir in white chocolate and nuts.

2 Onto ungreased cookie sheet, drop dough by rounded tablespoonfuls about 2 inches apart.

3 Bake 10 to 12 minutes or until light brown. Cool 1 to 2 minutes; remove from cookie sheet to cooling rack.

1 Cookie: Calories 190 (Calories from Fat 100); Total Fat 11g (Saturated Fat 4g); Cholesterol 15mg; Sodium 100mg; Total Carbohydrate 21g (Dietary Fiber 1g); Protein 2g

No macadamia nuts on hand? Use walnuts or peanuts instead.

Chocolate Drop Cookies

Prep Time: 25 min ▪ Start to Finish: 1 hr 25 min ▪ About 3 dozen cookies

Cookies
1 cup granulated sugar
$^1/_2$ cup butter or margarine, softened
$^1/_3$ cup buttermilk
1 teaspoon vanilla
1 large egg
2 oz unsweetened baking chocolate, melted and cooled
$1^3/_4$ cups all-purpose flour

$^1/_2$ teaspoon baking soda
$^1/_2$ teaspoon salt
1 cup chopped nuts, toasted if desired

Chocolate Frosting
2 oz unsweetened baking chocolate
2 tablespoons butter or margarine
2 cups powdered sugar
3 tablespoons hot water

1 Heat oven to 400°F. Grease cookie sheet with shortening or cooking spray, or line with cooking parchment paper or silicone baking mat.

2 In large bowl, beat granulated sugar, ½ cup butter, the buttermilk, vanilla, egg and chocolate with electric mixer on medium speed, or mix with spoon. Stir in flour, baking soda and salt. Stir in nuts.

3 Onto cookie sheet, drop dough by rounded tablespoonfuls about 2 inches apart.

4 Bake 8 to 10 minutes or until almost no indentation remains when touched in center. Immediately remove from cookie sheet to cooling rack. Cool completely, about 30 minutes.

5 In 2-quart saucepan, melt 2 oz chocolate and 2 tablespoons butter over low heat, stirring occasionally; remove from heat. Stir in powdered sugar and hot water until smooth. (If frosting is too thick, add more water, 1 teaspoon at a time. If frosting is too thin, add more powdered sugar, 1 tablespoon at a time.) Frost cookies.

1 Cookie: Calories 140 (Calories from Fat 65); Total Fat 7g (Saturated Fat 3g); Cholesterol 15mg; Sodium 75mg; Total Carbohydrate 18g (Dietary Fiber 1g); Protein 2g

Save preparation time—use your microwave to melt the chocolate for the cookie dough and the chocolate and butter for the frosting.

Chocolate Crinkles

Prep Time: 1 hr 35 min ■ Start to Finish: 5 hr 5 min ■ About 6 dozen cookies

2 cups granulated sugar
$1/2$ cup vegetable oil
2 teaspoons vanilla
4 oz unsweetened baking chocolate, melted, cooled
4 eggs
2 cups all-purpose flour
2 teaspoons baking powder
$1/2$ teaspoon salt
1 cup powdered sugar

1 In large bowl, mix granulated sugar, oil, vanilla and chocolate. Stir in eggs, one at a time. Stir in flour, baking powder and salt. Cover; refrigerate at least 3 hours.

2 Heat oven to 350°F. Grease cookie sheet with shortening or cooking spray. Place powdered sugar in small bowl. Drop dough by rounded teaspoonfuls into powdered sugar; roll in sugar to coat. Shape dough into balls. Place about 2 inches apart on cookie sheet.

3 Bake 10 to 12 minutes or until almost no indentation remains when touched. Remove from cookie sheet to cooling rack. Cool completely, about 30 minutes.

1 Cookie: Calories 70 (Calories from Fat 25); Total Fat 2.5g (Saturated Fat 1g); Cholesterol 10mg; Sodium 35mg; Total Carbohydrate 10g (Dietary Fiber 0g); Protein 0g

See photo on page 74.

Oatmeal-Raisin Cookies

Prep Time: 40 min ▪ Start to Finish: 40 min ▪ About 3 dozen cookies

²/₃ cup granulated sugar
²/₃ cup packed brown sugar
¹/₂ cup butter or margarine, softened
¹/₂ cup shortening
1 teaspoon baking soda
1 teaspoon ground cinnamon
1 teaspoon vanilla
¹/₂ teaspoon baking powder
¹/₂ teaspoon salt
2 eggs
3 cups quick-cooking or old-fashioned oats
1 cup all-purpose flour
1 cup raisins, chopped nuts or semisweet chocolate chips, if desired

1 Heat oven to 375°F. In large bowl, beat all ingredients except oats, flour and raisins with electric mixer on medium speed, or mix with spoon. Stir in oats, flour and raisins.

2 On ungreased cookie sheet, drop dough by rounded tablespoonfuls about 2 inches apart.

3 Bake 9 to 11 minutes or until light brown. Immediately remove from cookie sheet to cooling rack.

1 Cookie: Calories 120 (Calories from Fat 60); Total Fat 6g (Saturated Fat 2g); Cholesterol 20mg; Sodium 100mg; Total Carbohydrate 15g (Dietary Fiber 0g); Protein 2g

Quick-cooking and old-fashioned rolled oats are interchangeable unless a recipe calls for a specific type. Instant oatmeal products are not the same as quick-cooking or old-fashioned oats and should not be used for baking—you will get gummy or mushy results.

Spicy Pumpkin-Date Cookies

Prep Time: 40 min ■ Start to Finish: 40 min ■ About 4 dozen cookies

1 cup sugar
$\frac{1}{2}$ cup butter or margarine, softened
1 cup canned pumpkin
2 eggs
2 cups all-purpose flour
2 teaspoons baking powder
2 teaspoons ground cinnamon
$\frac{1}{2}$ teaspoon ground nutmeg
$\frac{1}{2}$ teaspoon ground ginger
$\frac{1}{4}$ teaspoon ground cloves
1 cup chopped dates
$\frac{1}{2}$ cup chopped walnuts

1 Heat oven to 375°F. In a large bowl, beat sugar and butter with electric mixer on medium speed until light and fluffy, or mix with spoon. Beat in pumpkin and eggs. Stir in remaining ingredients except dates and walnuts. Stir in dates and walnuts.

2 Drop dough by rounded teaspoonfuls about 2 inches apart onto ungreased cookie sheet. Bake 8 to 10 minutes or until edges are set. Immediately remove from cookie sheet to cooling rack.

1 Cookie: Calories 80 (Calories from Fat 25); Fat 3g (Saturated 1g); Cholesterol 10mg; Sodium 45mg; Total Carbohydrate 12g (Dietary Fiber 0g); Protein 1g

Old-Fashioned Rum-Raisin Cookies

Prep Time: 1 hr ▪ Start to Finish: 1 hr 30 min ▪ About 2¹/₂ dozen cookies

1 cup raisins
¹/₂ cup water
¹/₄ cup rum
³/₄ cup sugar
¹/₂ cup butter or margarine, softened
1 egg
1³/₄ cups all-purpose flour
¹/₂ teaspoon baking soda
¹/₂ teaspoon baking powder
¹/₄ teaspoon salt

1 In 1-quart saucepan, heat raisins, water and rum to boiling; reduce heat. Simmer uncovered 20 to 30 minutes or until raisins are plump and liquid has evaporated. Cool raisins 30 minutes.

2 Heat oven to 375°F. In large bowl, beat sugar and butter with electric mixer on medium speed about 3 minutes or until fluffy, or mix with spoon. Beat in egg. Stir in remaining ingredients. Stir in raisins.

3 Drop dough by rounded tablespoonfuls about 2 inches apart onto ungreased cookie sheet. Bake 9 to 11 minutes or until light brown. Remove from cookie sheet to cooling rack.

1 Cookie: Calories 90 (Calories from Fat 25); Total Fat 3g (Saturated 1g); Cholesterol 5mg; Sodium 85mg; Total Carbohydrate 15g (Dietary Fiber 0g); Protein 1g

Substitute 1 teaspoon rum extract mixed with ¼ cup water for the rum if you like.

Applesauce Jumbles

Prep Time: 20 min ∎ Start to Finish: 1 hr 30 min ∎ About 4½ to 5 dozen cookies

Cookies
2¾ cups all-purpose flour
1½ cups packed brown sugar
1 cup chopped nuts, if desired
1 cup raisins
¾ cup applesauce
½ cup butter or margarine, softened
1 teaspoon salt
1 teaspoon ground cinnamon
1 teaspoon vanilla

½ teaspoon baking soda
¼ teaspoon ground cloves
2 eggs

Browned Butter Glaze
⅓ cup butter (do not use margarine)
2 cups powdered sugar
1½ teaspoons vanilla
2 to 4 tablespoons hot water

1 In large bowl, mix all cookie ingredients with spoon. (If dough is soft, cover and refrigerate.)

2 Heat oven to 375°F. Onto ungreased cookie sheet, drop dough by rounded teaspoonfuls about 2 inches apart.

3 In 1-quart saucepan, melt ⅓ cup butter over low heat until golden brown. Remove from heat. Stir in powdered sugar and 1½ teaspoon vanilla. Stir in hot water until smooth and spreadable.

4 Bake about 10 minutes or until almost no indentation remains when touched. Immediately remove from cookie sheet to cooling rack. Cool completely, about 30 minutes. Spread with glaze.

1 Cookie: Calories 105 (Calories from Fat 25); Total Fat 3g (Saturated 2g); Cholesterol 15mg; Sodium 80mg; Total Carbohydrate 18g (Dietary Fiber 0g); Protein 1g

If you've never tasted Browned Butter Glaze, you're in for a treat. It's the ultimate in buttery flavor and teams well with this classic cookie.

See photo on page 31.

Raisin Crisscross Cookies

Prep time: 20 min ▪ Start to Finish: 30 min ▪ About 3 dozen cookies

3/4 cup sugar
1/4 cup shortening
1/4 cup margarine or butter, softened
1 egg
1/2 teaspoon lemon extract or vanilla
1 3/4 cups all-purpose flour
3/4 teaspoon cream of tartar
3/4 teaspoon baking soda
1/4 teaspoon salt
1 cup raisins

1 Heat oven to 400°F. In large bowl, mix sugar, shortening, margarine, egg and lemon extract. Stir in remaining ingredients.

2 Shape dough by rounded teaspoonfuls into balls. Place 3 inches apart on ungreased cookie sheet. Flatten in crisscross pattern with fork dipped in flour.

3 Bake 8 to 10 minutes or until light brown. Remove from cookie sheet to cooling rack.

1 Cookie: Calories 75 (Calories from Fat 25); Total Fat 3g (Saturated Fat 1g); Cholesterol 10mg; Sodium 55mg; Total Carbohydrate 12g (Dietary Fiber 0g); Protein 0g

A potato masher dipped into flour is another quick way to flatten these cookies.

Soft No-Roll Sugar Cookies

Prep Time: 20 min ▪ Start to Finish: 2 hr 50 min ▪ About 3½ dozen cookies

1½ cups granulated sugar
1 cup powdered sugar
1 cup butter or margarine, softened
¾ cup vegetable oil
2 tablespoons milk
1 tablespoon vanilla
2 eggs
4¼ cups all-purpose flour
1 teaspoon baking soda
1 teaspoon cream of tartar
½ teaspoon salt

1 In large bowl, beat 1 cup of the granulated sugar, the powdered sugar, butter, oil, milk, vanilla and eggs with electric mixer on medium speed, or mix with spoon. Stir in flour, baking soda, cream of tartar and salt. Cover; refrigerate about 2 hours or until firm.

2 Heat oven to 350°F. Shape dough into 1½-inch balls. In small bowl, place remaining ½ cup granulated sugar. Roll balls in sugar. On ungreased cookie sheet, place balls about 3 inches apart. Press bottom of drinking glass on each ball until about ¼ inch thick. If glass starts to stick, press bottom of glass on cookie dough as needed before pressing balls of dough (the fat in the dough helps to grease the bottom of the glass). Sprinkle each cookie with a little additional sugar.

3 Bake 13 to 15 minutes or until set and edges just begin to turn brown. Immediately remove from cookie sheet to cooling rack.

1 Cookie: Calories 160 (Calories from Fat 80); Total Fat 9g (Saturated Fat 3g); Cholesterol 20mg; Sodium 90mg; Total Carbohydrate 20g (Dietary Fiber 0g); Protein 2g

Brown Sugar Refrigerator Cookies

Prep Time: 20 min ▪ Start to Finish: 2 hr 55 min ▪ About 6 dozen cookies

1 cup packed brown sugar
1 cup butter or margarine, softened
1 teaspoon vanilla
1 large egg
3 cups all-purpose flour
$1^{1}/_{2}$ teaspoons ground cinnamon
$^{1}/_{2}$ teaspoon baking soda
$^{1}/_{2}$ teaspoon salt
$^{1}/_{3}$ cup finely chopped nuts

1 In large bowl, beat brown sugar, butter, vanilla and egg with electric mixer on medium speed, or mix with spoon. Stir in remaining ingredients except nuts. Stir in nuts.

2 Shape dough into 10 × 3-inch rectangle on plastic wrap. Wrap and refrigerate about 2 hours or until firm, but no longer than 24 hours.

3 Heat oven to 375°F. Cut rectangle into ⅛-inch slices. On ungreased cookie sheet, place slices 2 inches apart.

4 Bake 6 to 8 minutes or until light brown. Cool 1 to 2 minutes; remove from cookie sheet to cooling rack.

1 Cookie: Calories 60 (Calories from fat 25); Total Fat 3g (Saturated Fat 2g); Cholesterol 10mg; Sodium 45mg; Total Carbohydrate 7g (Dietary Fiber 0g); Protein 1g

You can call these refrigerator or freezer cookies. Freeze the tightly wrapped cookie dough for up to 2 months, then slice and bake when you want. Just add 1 or 2 minutes to the baking time when the dough comes straight from the freezer.

Maple-Nut Refrigerator Cookies

Prep Time: 20 min ■ Start to Finish: 2 hr 30 min ■ About 4 dozen cookies

$^3/_4$ cup packed brown sugar

$^3/_4$ cup butter or margarine, softened

$^1/_4$ teaspoon maple extract

$1^1/_2$ cups all-purpose flour

1 teaspoon baking powder

$^1/_4$ teaspoon salt

1 cup chopped pecans

1 Beat brown sugar, butter and maple extract in large bowl with electric mixer on medium speed, or mix with spoon. Stir in flour, baking powder and salt. Stir in pecans. Shape into roll, 12 inches long. Wrap and refrigerate about 2 hours or until firm.

2 Heat oven to 375°F. Cut roll into ¼-inch slices. Place 2 inches apart on ungreased cookie sheet. Bake 8 to 10 minutes or until edges are golden brown. Remove from cookie sheet to cooling rack.

1 Cookie: Calories 75 (Calories from Fat 45); Fat 5g (Saturated Fat 1g); Cholesterol 0mg; Sodium 55mg; Total Carbohydrate 7g (Dietary Fiber 0g); Protein 1g

Joe Froggers

Prep Time: 20 min ∎ Start to Finish: 40 min ∎ About 3 dozen cookies

1 cup sugar
$^1/_2$ cup shortening
1 cup dark molasses
$^1/_2$ cup water
4 cups all-purpose flour
$1^1/_2$ teaspoons salt
$1^1/_2$ teaspoons ground ginger
1 teaspoon baking soda
$^1/_2$ teaspoon ground cloves
$^1/_2$ teaspoon ground nutmeg
$^1/_4$ teaspoon ground allspice

1 In 3-quart bowl, mix 1 cup sugar, the shortening, molasses and water. Stir in remaining ingredients. Cover and refrigerate at least 2 hours.

2 Heat oven to 375°F. Roll dough $^1/_4$ inch thick on well-floured cloth-covered surface. Cut into 3-inch rounds; sprinkle with sugar. Place about $1^1/_2$ inches apart on ungreased cookie sheet.

3 Bake 10 to 12 minutes or until almost no indentation remains when touched. Cool 2 minutes; remove from cookie sheet to cooling rack. Cool completely.

1 Cookie: Calories 123 (Calories from Fat 25); Total Fat 3g (Saturated Fat 1g); Cholesterol 0mg; Sodium 137mg; Total Carbohydrate 23g (Dietary Fiber 0g); Protein 1g

Ginger Shortbread Wedges

Prep Time: 10 min ■ Start to Finish: 40 min ■ 16 cookies

$^2/_3$ cup butter or margarine, softened
$^1/_3$ cup powdered sugar
3 tablespoons finely chopped crystallized ginger
$1^1/_3$ cups all-purpose flour
2 teaspoons granulated sugar

1 Heat oven to 350°F. In large bowl, beat butter, powdered sugar and ginger with electric mixer on medium speed, or mix with spoon. Stir in flour.

2 On ungreased cookie sheet, pat dough into 9-inch round. Sprinkle with granulated sugar. Bake about 20 minutes or until golden brown. Cool 10 minutes. Cut into 16 wedges.

1 Cookie: Calories 125 (Calories from Fat 70); Total Fat 8g (Saturated 2g); Cholesterol 0mg; Sodium 90mg; Total Carbohydrate 12g (Dietary Fiber 0g); Protein 1g.

These cookies are delicious as is but can be dressed up by dipping them in melted chocolate or candy coating. After dipping cookies, place on a cooling rack to set.

Cream Squares

Prep Time: 20 min ▪ Start to Finish: 2 hr 50 min ▪ About 4 dozen cookies

2 eggs
1 cup sugar
1 cup heavy whipping cream
4 cups all-purpose flour
3 teaspoons baking powder
1 teaspoon salt

1 In large bowl, beat eggs with electric mixer on medium speed until foamy. Gradually beat in sugar. Stir in whipping cream. Stir in flour, baking powder and salt. Cover and refrigerate about 2 hours or until firm.

2 Heat oven to 375°F. Grease cookie sheet. Roll half of dough at a time into 12 × 8-inch rectangle, on lightly floured surface. Cut into 2-inch squares. Place 2 inches apart on cookie sheet. Make two ½-inch cuts on all sides of each square. Bake 10 to 13 minutes or until edges are light brown. Remove from cookie sheet to cooling rack.

1 Cookie: Calories 70 (Calories from Fat 20); Total Fat 2g (Saturated 1g); Cholesterol 15mg; Sodium 85mg; Total Carbohydrate 12g (Dietary Fiber 0g); Protein 1g

Chocolate Chip Cream Squares: Stir ½ cup mini chocolate chips into dough.

Pecan Crisps

Prep Time: 20 min ▪ Start to Finish: 50 min ▪ About 4 dozen cookies

2 cups sugar
¾ cup very finely chopped pecans
⅓ cup butter or margarine, softened
1 teaspoon vanilla
2 eggs
2¼ cups all-purpose flour
2½ teaspoons baking powder
¼ teaspoon salt

1 In large bowl, heat oven to 375°F. Mix sugar and pecans; reserve ¾ cup. Beat butter, vanilla and eggs into remaining sugar mixture with electric mixer on low speed, or mix with spoon. Stir in flour, baking powder and salt.

2 Roll dough into 18 × 13-inch rectangle on lightly floured surface. Sprinkle with reserved sugar mixture. Press sugar mixture into dough with rolling pin. Cut dough diagonally every 2 inches in both directions with pastry wheel or knife to form diamonds. Place about 2 inches apart on ungreased cookie sheet. Bake 8 to 10 minutes or until golden brown. Immediately remove from cookie sheet to cooling rack.

1 Cookie: Calories 85 (Calories from Fat 25); Total Fat 3g (Saturated 0g); Cholesterol 10mg; Sodium 55mg; Total Carbohydrate 13g (Dietary Fiber 0g); Protein 1g

Lemon Squares

Prep Time: 25 min ▪ Start to Finish: 2 hr 20 min ▪ 25 squares

1 cup all-purpose flour
$\frac{1}{2}$ cup butter or margarine, softened
$\frac{1}{4}$ cup powdered sugar, plus additional for sprinkling
1 cup granulated sugar
2 teaspoons grated lemon peel, if desired
2 tablespoons lemon juice
$\frac{1}{2}$ teaspoon baking powder
$\frac{1}{4}$ teaspoon salt
2 eggs

1 Heat oven to 350°F. In small bowl, mix flour, butter and powdered sugar. Press in ungreased 8-inch pan, building up ½-inch edge. Bake 20 minutes.

2 In small bowl, beat remaining ingredients with electric mixer on high speed about 3 minutes or until light and fluffy. Pour over hot crust.

3 Bake 25 to 30 minutes longer or until almost no indentation remains when touched lightly in center. Cool completely, about 1 hour. Sprinkle with additional powdered sugar. For squares, cut into 5 rows by 5 rows.

1 Square: Calories 90 (Calories from Fat 35); Total Fat 4g (Saturated Fat 2g); Cholesterol 25mg; Sodium 65mg; Total Carbohydrate 13g (Dietary Fiber 0g); Protein 1g

Applesauce Jumbles (page 20)
and Lemon Squares

Caramel Apple-Nut Bars

Prep Time: 15 min ▪ Start to Finish: 2 hr 20 min ▪ 36 bars

2 cups all-purpose flour
2 cups quick-cooking oats
1¹/₂ cups packed brown sugar
1¹/₄ cups butter or margarine, softened
1 teaspoon baking soda
¹/₂ teaspoon salt
¹/₂ cup caramel topping
3 tablespoons all-purpose flour
1 medium apple, peeled and chopped (1 cup)
¹/₂ cup coarsely chopped pecans

1 Heat oven to 350°F. Grease bottom and sides of 13 × 9-inch pan with shortening or cooking spray. In large bowl, beat 2 cups flour, the oats, brown sugar, baking soda, salt and butter with electric mixer on low speed, or mix with spoon, until crumbly. Press about 3 cups of the mixture in pan. Bake 10 minutes.

2 Meanwhile, in small bowl, mix caramel topping and 3 tablespoons flour. Sprinkle apple and pecans over partially baked crust. Drizzle with caramel mixture. Sprinkle with remaining crust mixture.

3 Bake 20 to 25 minutes or until golden brown. Cool completely, about 1 hour 30 minutes. For bars, cut into 6 rows by 6 rows.

1 Bar: Calories 160 (Calories from Fat 70); Total Fat 8g (Saturated Fat 4); Cholesterol 15mg; Sodium 130mg; Total Carbohydrate 21g (Dietary Fiber 0g); Protein 2g

Date-Apricot Bars

Prep Time: 25 min ▪ Start to Finish: 55 min ▪ About 40 bars

Bars
½ cup butter or margarine, softened
1 cup packed brown sugar
1½ cups all-purpose flour
1 teaspoon salt
½ teaspoon baking soda
1 cup old-fashioned or quick-cooking oats
½ cup chopped walnuts or almonds

Date-Apricot Filling
1½ cups cut-up dates
1½ cups cut-up dried apricots
¼ cup sugar
1½ cups water

1 In 1½-quart saucepan, heat all filling ingredients to boiling, stirring constantly; reduce heat. Simmer uncovered about 10 minutes, stirring occasionally, until thickened. Set aside to cool.

2 Heat oven to 400°F. Grease bottom and sides of 13 × 9-inch pan with shortening or spray with cooking spray. In large bowl, mix butter and brown sugar with spoon. Stir in flour, salt, baking soda and oats. Press half of the crumbly mixture in pan. Spread filling over top. Sprinkle with walnuts. Sprinkle with remaining crumbly mixture; press lightly.

3 Bake 25 to 30 minutes or until light brown. While warm, make 1 diagonal cut from corner to corner. Continue cutting parallel to first cut, each about 1½ inches apart. Repeat, cutting diagonally in opposite direction.

1 Bar: Calories 120 (Calories from Fat 35); Total Fat 4g (Saturated Fat 2g); Cholesterol 5mg; Sodium 95mg; Total Carbohydrate 20g (Dietary Fiber 1g); Protein 1g

Such versatile bars! You can omit the apricots in the filling and just use 3 cups dates, or use half dates and half raisins. If you're feeling adventurous, you can try other dried fruit combinations, like mango-apricot, date-pineapple or any combination you like.

Saucepan Granola Bars

Prep Time: 10 min ■ Start to Finish: 1 hr 35 min ■ 48 bars

$1/2$ cup butter or margarine
$2^1/2$ cups Original Bisquick® mix
2 cups granola with fruit
1 cup packed brown sugar
$1/2$ cup chopped nuts
1 teaspoon vanilla
2 eggs

1 Heat oven to 375°F. In 3-quart saucepan, melt butter over low heat. Stir in remaining ingredients until blended. In ungreased 13 × 9-inch pan, spread mixture evenly.

2 Bake 20 to 25 minutes or until deep golden brown. Cool completely, about 1 hour. For bars, cut into 8 rows by 6 rows.

1 Bar: Calories 90 (Calories from Fat 40); Total Fat 5g (Saturated Fat 2g); Cholesterol 15mg; Sodium 110mg; Total Carbohydrate 11g (Dietary Fiber 0g); Protein 1g

Drizzle cooled bars with melted chocolate chips for a pretty and tasty finish.

Salted Nut Bars

Prep Time: 20 min ▪ Start to Finish: 40 min ▪ 32 bars

1½ cups all-purpose flour
¾ cup packed brown sugar
¼ teaspoon salt
½ cup butter or margarine, softened
2 cups salted mixed nuts or peanuts
1 cup butterscotch-flavored chips
½ cup light corn syrup
2 tablespoons butter or margarine

1 Heat oven to 350°F. In medium bowl, mix flour, brown sugar and salt. Cut in ½ cup butter, using pastry blender (or pulling 2 table knives through ingredients in opposite directions), until evenly mixed.

2 In bottom of ungreased 13 × 9-inch pan, press dough evenly. Bake 15 minutes; cool slightly.

3 Cut up any large nuts. Sprinkle nuts evenly over crust. In 1-quart saucepan, heat remaining ingredients over low heat, stirring occasionally, just until chips are melted. Drizzle butterscotch mixture evenly over nuts. Bake 5 minutes longer. For bars, cut into 8 rows by 4 rows while warm for easiest cutting.

1 Bar: Calories 150 (Calories from Fat 80); Total Fat 9g (Saturated Fat 3g); Cholesterol 10mg; Sodium 110mg; Total Carbohydrate 15g (Dietary Fiber 1g); Protein 2g

Love sweet and salty together? Then this yummy and easy-to-put-together bar cookie is made just for you. Delicious anytime, these bars are very popular—during the holidays we get a great many requests for this scrumptious recipe.

Thumbprint Cookies

Mocha Cookies

Chocolate Shortbread

Cream Wafers

Butterscotch Shortbread

Old-Fashioned Molasses Cookies

Key Lime Coolers

Lemon Stampers

Lemon Cookie Tarts

Citrus Biscotti

Cinnamon Twists

Raspberry Logs

Russian Tea Cakes

Cappuccino-Pistachio Shortbread

Hazelnut Biscotti

Rum-Cashew Biscotti

Almond Biscotti

Almond Bonbons

2

classic cookies

Thumbprint Cookies

Prep Time: 1 hr ▪ Start to Finish: 1 hr ▪ About 3 dozen cookies

¼ cup packed brown sugar
¼ cup shortening
¼ cup butter or margarine, softened
½ teaspoon vanilla
1 egg yolk
1 cup all-purpose flour

¼ teaspoon salt
1 egg white
1 cup finely chopped nuts
About 6 tablespoons jelly or jam
(any flavor)

1 Heat oven to 350°F. In medium bowl, beat brown sugar, shortening, butter, vanilla and egg yolk with electric mixer on medium speed, or mix with spoon. Stir in flour and salt.

2 Shape dough into 1-inch balls. In small bowl, beat egg white slightly with fork. Place nuts in another small bowl. Dip each ball into egg white, then roll in nuts. On ungreased cookie sheet, place balls about 1 inch apart. Press thumb or end of wooden spoon into center of each cookie to make indentation, but do not press all the way to cookie sheet.

3 Bake about 10 minutes or until light brown. Quickly remake indentations with end of wooden spoon if necessary. Immediately remove from cookie sheet to cooling rack. Fill each thumbprint with about ½ teaspoon jelly.

1 Cookie: Calories 80 (Calories from Fat 45); Total Fat 5g (Saturated Fat 1.5g); Cholesterol 10mg; Sodium 30mg; Total Carbohydrate 7g (Dietary Fiber 0g); Protein 1g

Fudgy Peanut Cookies: Roll balls of dough in finely chopped salted dry-roasted peanuts. Cool cookies completely. Fill indentations with purchased hot fudge topping or hazelnut spread with cocoa (from 13-oz jar) instead of the jelly.

Lemon-Almond Thumbprint Cookies: Roll balls of dough in finely chopped slivered almonds. Fill indentations with Lemon Curd (page 151) or purchased lemon curd instead of the jelly.

Mocha Cookies

Prep Time: 25 min ▪ Start to Finish: 1 hr 40 min ▪ About 2½ dozen cookies

Cookies

1 egg

2 tablespoons instant coffee crystals

1 cup granulated sugar

½ cup butter or margarine, softened

1½ teaspoons vanilla

1½ cups all-purpose flour

½ cup baking cocoa

¼ teaspoon baking powder

¼ teaspoon baking soda

¼ teaspoon salt

Caramel Drizzle

1¾ cups powdered sugar

¼ cup caramel topping

½ teaspoon vanilla

About 2 tablespoons milk

1 In medium bowl, beat egg and coffee crystals with electric mixer on medium speed until crystals dissolve. Add granulated sugar, butter and 1½ teaspoons vanilla. Beat on medium speed until light and fluffy. Stir in remaining cookie ingredients. Cover and refrigerate at least 1 hour until chilled.

2 Heat oven to 375°F. Roll dough ⅛ inch thick on lightly floured surface. Cut with 2½-inch cookie cutters. On ungreased cookie sheet, place shapes about 1 inch apart. Bake about 7 minutes or until set. Cool 1 minute; remove from cookie sheet to cooling rack. Cool completely, about 30 minutes.

3 In small bowl, mix powdered sugar, caramel topping and vanilla until crumbly. Stir in just enough milk until smooth and thin enough to drizzle. Drizzle over cookies.

1 Cookie: Calories 120 (Calories from Fat 30); Total Fat 3.5g (Saturated Fat 1.5g); Cholesterol 15mg; Sodium 65mg; Total Carbohydrate. 21g (Dietary Fiber 0g); Protein 1g

Chocolate Shortbread

Prep Time: 1 hr ▪ Start to Finish: 1 hr ▪ About 4 dozen cookies

Shortbread

2 cups powdered sugar

1 1/2 cups butter or margarine, softened

3 cups all-purpose flour

3/4 cup baking cocoa

2 teaspoons vanilla

4 oz semisweet baking chocolate, melted
    and cooled

1/2 teaspoon shortening

Creamy Frosting

3 cups powdered sugar

1/3 cup butter or margarine, softened

1 1/2 teaspoons vanilla

About 2 tablespoons milk

1 Heat oven to 325°F. In large bowl, beat powdered sugar and butter with electric mixer on medium speed until light and fluffy, or mix with spoon. Stir in flour, cocoa and vanilla.

2 Roll half of dough at a time 1/2 inch thick on lightly floured surface. Cut into 3-inch rounds. Place 2 inches apart on ungreased cookie sheet. Bake 9 to 11 minutes or until firm (cookies should not be dark brown). Remove from cookie sheet to cooling rack. Cool completely.

3 In small bowl, mix chocolate and shortening until smooth. In medium bowl, mix 3 cups powdered sugar and butter. Stir in 1 1/2 teaspoons vanilla and the milk. Beat with spoon until smooth and spreadable.

4 Spread each cookie with about 1 teaspoon frosting. Immediately make 3 concentric circles on frosting with melted chocolate. Starting at center, pull a toothpick through chocolate circles to make spider web design. Let stand until chocolate is firm.

1 Cookie: Calories 160 (Calories from Fat 80); Total Fat 9g (Saturated Fat 2g); Cholesterol 0mg; Sodium 85mg; Total Carbohydrate 20g (Dietary Fiber 1g); Protein 1g

Another idea for a quick cookie design is to drizzle straight lines of chocolate across the frosting, then pull a wooden toothpick back and forth across the lines to create scalloped effect.

Cream Wafers

Prep Time: 10 min ▪ Start to Finish: 1 hr 30 min ▪ About 5 dozen cookies

Cookies
1 cup butter or margarine, softened
⅓ cup heavy whipping cream
2 cups all-purpose flour
Granulated sugar

Cream Filling
¼ cup butter or margarine, softened
¾ cup powdered sugar
1 teaspoon vanilla
Food color

1 In medium bowl, mix 1 cup butter, whipping cream and flour thoroughly with spoon. Cover and refrigerate at least 1 hour.

2 Heat oven to 375°F. On lightly floured surface, roll about ⅓ of the dough at a time until ⅛ inch thick (keep remaining dough refrigerated until ready to roll). Cut into 1½-inch rounds.

3 Cover a piece of waxed paper with a thick layer of granulated sugar. Transfer rounds with spatula to sugar-covered waxed paper; turn each round so that both sides are coated with sugar. On ungreased cookie sheet, place rounds about 1 inch apart. Prick rounds with fork about 4 times.

4 Bake 7 to 9 minutes or just until set but not brown. Remove from cookie sheet to cooling rack. Cool completely, about 30 minutes. Meanwhile, in small bowl, beat ¼ cup butter, powdered sugar and vanilla with spoon until smooth and fluffy. Stir in a few drops of food color. (A few drops of water can be added if necessary to make filling spreadable.) Put cookies together in pairs (bottoms together) with filling.

1 Cookie: Calories 60 (Calories from Fat 35); Total Fat 4g (Saturated Fat 3g); Cholesterol 10mg; Sodium 25mg; Total Carbohydrate 6g (Dietary Fiber 0g); Protein 0g

Butterscotch Shortbread

Prep Time: 20 min ■ Start to Finish: 45 min ■ About 2 dozen cookies

¹/₄ cup butter or margarine, softened
¹/₄ cup shortening
¹/₄ cup packed brown sugar
2 tablespoons granulated sugar
1 cup plus 2 tablespoons all-purpose flour
¹/₄ teaspoon salt

1 Heat oven to 300°F. In large bowl, beat butter, shortening and sugars with electric mixer on medium speed until creamy, or mix with spoon. Stir in flour and salt. (Dough will be dry and crumbly; use hands to mix completely.)

2 On lightly floured surface, roll dough into 9 × 6-inch rectangle. Cut into 1½-inch squares. On ungreased cookie sheet, place squares about 1 inch apart.

3 Bake about 25 minutes or until set. Remove from cookie sheet to cooling rack; cool.

1 Cookie: Calories 70 (Calories from Fat 35); Total Fat 4g (Saturated Fat 2g); Cholesterol 5mg; Sodium 40mg; Total Carbohydrate 8g (Dietary Fiber 0g); Protein 1g

Watch the clock when baking these cookies because they brown very little, and the shape does not change.

Old-Fashioned Molasses Cookies

Prep Time: 25 min ■ Start to Finish: 5 hr 20 min ■ About 6 dozen cookies

Cookies
1½ cups granulated sugar
1 cup butter or margarine, softened
½ cup molasses
2 eggs
3 teaspoons baking soda
½ cup water
5½ cups all-purpose flour
1½ teaspoons ground cinnamon
1 teaspoon ground ginger
1 teaspoon ground cloves
1 teaspoon salt

Vanilla Cooked Frosting
1 envelope plus 2 teaspoons
    unflavored gelatin
1 cup cold water
1 cup granulated sugar
2¼ cups powdered sugar
1½ teaspoons vanilla
1 teaspoon baking powder
⅛ teaspoon salt

1 In large bowl, mix 1½ cups granulated sugar, butter, molasses and eggs with spoon. In small bowl, dissolve baking soda in ½ cup water; stir into molasses mixture. Stir in remaining cookie ingredients. Cover and refrigerate at least 2 hours.

2 Heat oven to 375°F. Lightly grease cookie sheet with shortening. On lightly floured surface, roll dough ¼ inch thick. Cut with floured 2¾-inch round cutter. On cookie sheet, place cutouts about 2 inches apart.

3 Bake 8 to 10 minutes or until light brown. Remove from cookie sheet to cooling rack. Cool completely, about 30 minutes.

4 Meanwhile, in 2-quart saucepan, sprinkle gelatin on 1 cup cold water to soften; stir in 1 cup granulated sugar. Heat to a rolling boil; reduce heat. Simmer uncovered 10 minutes. Place powdered sugar in large bowl. Pour hot mixture over powdered sugar; beat with electric mixer on medium speed about 2 minutes or until foamy. Beat in vanilla, baking powder and ⅛ teaspoon salt on high speed 12 to 15 minutes or until soft peaks form.

5 Frost bottoms of cookies with vanilla frosting. Let stand 2 to 3 hours before storing to allow frosting to dry.

1 Cookie: Calories 110 (Calories from Fat 25); Total Fat 3g (Saturated Fat 2g); Cholesterol 15mg; Sodium 115mg; Total Carbohydrate 20g (Dietary Fiber 0g); Protein 1g

Key Lime Coolers

Prep Time: 10 min ▪ Start to Finish: 1 hr 30 min ▪ About 4 dozen cookies

Cookies

1 cup butter or margarine, softened

1/2 cup powdered sugar

1 3/4 cups all-purpose flour

1/4 cup cornstarch

1 tablespoon grated lime peel

1/2 teaspoon vanilla

Granulated sugar

Key Lime Glaze

1/2 cup powdered sugar

2 teaspoons grated lime peel

4 teaspoons Key lime or regular
      lime juice

1 Heat oven to 350°F. In large bowl, beat butter and powdered sugar with electric mixer on medium speed until light and fluffy, or mix with spoon. Stir in flour, cornstarch, 1 tablespoon lime peel and vanilla until well blended.

2 Shape dough into 1-inch balls. On ungreased cookie sheet, place balls about 2 inches apart. Press bottom of glass into dough to grease, then dip into granulated sugar; press on shaped dough until 1/4 inch thick.

3 Bake 9 to 11 minutes or until edges are light golden brown. Remove from cookie sheet to cooling rack. Cool completely, about 30 minutes. Meanwhile, in small bowl, mix all glaze ingredients with spoon until smooth. Brush cookies with glaze.

1 Cookie: Calories 70 (Calories from Fat 35); Total Fat 4g (Saturated Fat 2g); Cholesterol 10mg; Sodium 25mg; Total Carbohydrate 8g (Dietary Fiber 0g); Protein 1g

These cookies, made with Key lime juice and peel, pack fresh, modern flavor. If you like using a cookie press, try making Key Lime Ribbons. Prepare dough as directed, but do not shape into balls. Place dough in cookie press fitted with a ribbon tip. Form long ribbons of dough on ungreased cookie sheet. Cut into 3-inch lengths. Continue as directed.

Lemon Stampers

Prep Time: 1 hr ▪ Start to Finish: 3 hr 40 min ▪ About 5 dozen cookies

1 cup butter or margarine, softened
1 package (3 oz) cream cheese, softened
¹/₂ cup sugar
1 tablespoon grated lemon peel
2 cups all-purpose flour

1 In large bowl, beat butter and cream cheese with electric mixer on medium speed, or mix with spoon. Stir in sugar and lemon peel. Gradually stir in flour. Cover; refrigerate about 2 hours or until firm.

2 Heat oven to 375°F. Shape dough into 1-inch balls. On ungreased cookie sheet, place balls about 2 inches apart. "Stamp" balls to about ¼-inch thickness using a potato masher, the bottom of a glass, the bumpy side of a meat mallet, the end of an empty spool of thread or a cookie press, dipping first into additional sugar.

3 Bake 7 to 9 minutes or until set but not brown. Remove from cookie sheet to cooling rack. Cool completely, about 30 minutes.

1 Cookie: Calories 50 (Calories from Fat 30); Total Fat 3.5g (Saturated Fat 2g); Cholesterol 10mg; Sodium 25mg; Total Carbohydrate 5g (Dietary Fiber 0g); Protein 0g

Lemon Cookie Tarts

Prep Time: 4 hr 50 min ■ Start to Finish: 4 hr 50 min ■ About 4 dozen cookies

Cookies

1 cup butter or margarine, softened
1/2 cup granulated sugar
1/2 teaspoon vanilla
1 egg
2 cups all-purpose flour
1/4 teaspoon salt

Lemon Filling

3 eggs
1 1/2 cups granulated sugar
3 tablespoons all-purpose flour
1/2 teaspoon baking powder
2 teaspoons grated lemon peel
2 tablespoons lemon juice
1 tablespoon powdered sugar,
    if desired

1 In large bowl, beat butter, 1/2 cup granulated sugar, the vanilla and 1 egg with electric mixer on medium speed, or mix with spoon. Stir in 2 cups flour and the salt. Cover; refrigerate about 1 hour or until firm.

2 Meanwhile, in small bowl, beat all filling ingredients except powdered sugar with electric mixer on medium speed, or mix with whisk. Cover; refrigerate.

3 Heat oven to 350°F. Spray 48 mini muffin cups with cooking spray. Shape dough into 48 one-inch balls. Place 1 ball in each muffin cup. Press dough into bottom and up side of cup. Spoon slightly less than 1 tablespoon filling into each cup.

4 Bake 18 to 20 minutes or until centers are puffed and edges are light brown. Cool in pan 30 minutes. With tip of knife, lift tarts from muffin cups to cooling rack; cool completely. Just before serving, sprinkle tarts with powdered sugar.

1 Cookie: Calories 90 (Calories from Fat 40); Total Fat 4.5g (Saturated Fat 2g); Cholesterol 30mg; Sodium 50mg; Total Carbohydrate 13g (Dietary Fiber 0g); Protein 1g

See photo on page 74.

Citrus Biscotti

Prep Time: 25 min ■ Total: 5 hr 5 min ■ About 30 biscotti

Biscotti
1 package (1 lb 2.25 oz) lemon cake mix with pudding in the mix
1 tablespoon vegetable oil
2 eggs
2 tablespoons grated lemon peel
1 tablespoon grated lime peel
1 tablespoon grated orange peel

Easy Lemon Glaze
1/4 cup lemon creamy ready-to-spread frosting (from 1-lb container)
2 to 4 teaspoons lemon juice

1 Heat oven to 350°F. In large bowl, mix all biscotti ingredients with spoon until dough forms.

2 On large ungreased cookie sheet, shape dough into 14 × 3-inch rectangle, 1/2 inch thick. Bake 20 to 25 minutes or until golden brown. Cool on cookie sheet on wire rack 15 minutes.

3 Cut dough crosswise into 1/2-inch slices. Arrange slices cut side up on cookie sheet. Bake 7 to 8 minutes or until bottoms are light golden brown; turn slices over. Bake 7 to 8 minutes longer or until bottoms are light golden brown. Cool 5 minutes; remove from cookie sheet to cooling rack. Cool completely, about 15 minutes.

4 Mix all glaze ingredients until thin enough to drizzle. Drizzle glaze over tops of biscotti. Let stand about 4 hours or until glaze is set.

1 Biscotti: Calories 100 (Calories from Fat 25); Total Fat 3g (Saturated Fat 1g); Cholesterol 15mg; Sodium 125mg; Total Carbohydrate 16g (Dietary Fiber 0g); Protein 1g

Try these biscotti with a cup of hot citrus-flavored tea—and yes, dunking is allowed!

Cinnamon Twists

Prep Time: 1 hr 30 min ▪ Start to Finish: 1 hr 30 min ▪ About 4 dozen cookies

1 cup sugar
1/2 cup butter or margarine, softened
2 teaspoons vanilla
1 egg
1 3/4 cups all-purpose flour
2 teaspoons baking powder
1/2 teaspoon salt
1 teaspoon ground cinnamon

1 Heat oven to 375°F. In large bowl, beat sugar, butter, vanilla and egg with electric mixer on medium speed, or mix with spoon. Stir in flour, baking powder and salt. Divide dough in half. Stir cinnamon into one half.

2 Shape 1 level teaspoonful each, plain and cinnamon dough, into 3-inch rope. Place ropes side by side; twist gently. Repeat with remaining dough. Place twists about 2 inches apart on ungreased cookie sheet. Bake 8 to 10 minutes or until very light brown. Remove from cookie sheet to cooling rack.

1 Cookie: Calories 55 (Calories from Fat 20); Total Fat 2g (Saturated Fat 0g); Cholesterol 5mg; Sodium 70mg; Total Carbohydrate 8g (Dietary Fiber 0g); Protein 1g

Cinnamon Knots: Prepare dough as directed except use 2 teaspoonfuls dough from each half to create 6-inch ropes. Place ropes side by side; twist gently and tie into knots. Bake as directed.

Raspberry Logs

Prep Time: 30 min ▪ Start to Finish: 3 hr 30 min ▪ 4 dozen cookies

1 cup granulated sugar
1/2 cup butter or margarine
1/4 cup shortening
2 teaspoons vanilla
2 eggs
2 1/4 cups all-purpose flour
1/2 cup ground walnuts
1 teaspoon baking powder
1/4 teaspoon salt
1/2 cup raspberry preserves
Powdered sugar

1 In large bowl, beat granulated sugar, butter, shortening, vanilla and eggs with electric mixer on medium speed, or mix with spoon. Stir in flour, walnuts, baking powder and salt. Cover and refrigerate about 3 hours or until firm.

2 Heat oven to 375°F. Roll half of dough at a time into 12-inch square on floured cloth-covered surface. Cut into 2 × 3-inch rectangles. Spoon 1/2 teaspoon preserves along one 3-inch side of each rectangle to within 1/4 inch of edge. Fold dough over preserves, beginning at 3-inch side. Seal edges with fork. Place on ungreased cookie sheet. Bake 8 to 10 minutes or until light brown. Remove from cookie sheet to cooling rack. Roll in powdered sugar while warm.

1 Cookie: Calories 90 (Calories from Fat 35); Total Fat 4g (Saturated Fat 1g); Cholesterol 10mg; Sodium 50mg; Total Carbohydrate 12g (Dietary Fiber 0g); Protein 1g

You can easily replace raspberry preserves with strawberry preserves, and if you prefer pecans, use them instead of the walnuts.

Top to bottom: Peppermint Tea Cakes,
Russian Tea Cakes and Lemon Tea Cakes

Russian Tea Cakes

Prep Time: 1 hr 5 min ▪ Start to Finish: 1 hr 35 min ▪ About 4 dozen cookies

1 cup butter or margarine, softened
$1/2$ cup powdered sugar
1 teaspoon vanilla
$2^{1}/_{4}$ cups all-purpose flour
$1/4$ teaspoon salt
$3/4$ cup finely chopped nuts
Additional powdered sugar

1 Heat oven to 400°F. In large bowl, beat butter, ½ cup powdered sugar and the vanilla with electric mixer on medium speed, or mix with spoon. Stir in flour and salt. Stir in nuts.

2 Shape dough by rounded teaspoonfuls into 1-inch balls. On ungreased cookie sheet, place balls about 2 inches apart.

3 Bake 8 to 9 minutes or until set but not brown. In small bowl, place additional powdered sugar. Immediately remove cookies from cookie sheet; roll in powdered sugar. Cool completely on cooling rack, about 30 minutes. Roll in powdered sugar again.

1 Cookie: Calories 80 (Calories from Fat 45); Total Fat 5g (Saturated Fat 2g); Cholesterol 10mg; Sodium 40mg; Total Carbohydrate 8g (Dietary Fiber 0g); Protein 0g

Lemon Tea Cakes: Substitute lemon extract for the vanilla and add 1 teaspoon grated lemon peel with the flour. Crush ½ cup lemon drops in food processor or blender. Stir in ¼ cup of the crushed lemon drops with the flour; reserve remaining candy. Bake as directed. Immediately roll baked cookies in powdered sugar; wait 10 minutes, then roll in reserved crushed lemon drops. Reroll, if desired.

Peppermint Tea Cakes: Crush ¾ cup hard peppermint candies in food processor or blender. Stir in ¼ cup of the crushed candies with the flour; reserve remaining candy. Bake as directed. Immediately roll baked cookies in powdered sugar; wait 10 minutes, then roll in reserved crushed candy. Reroll, if desired.

Cappuccino-Pistachio Shortbread

Prep Time: 1 hr ▪ Start to Finish: 1 hr ▪ 32 cookies

2 tablespoons cappuccino-flavored instant coffee mix (dry)

1 tablespoon water

¾ cup butter or margarine, softened

½ cup powdered sugar

2 cups all-purpose flour

½ cup chopped pistachio nuts

1 oz semisweet baking chocolate or white chocolate baking bar

1 teaspoon shortening

1 Heat oven to 350°F. In medium bowl, dissolve coffee mix in water. Add butter and powdered sugar. Beat with electric mixer on medium speed until creamy, or mix with spoon. Stir in flour and nuts, using hands if necessary, until stiff dough forms.

2 Divide dough in half. Shape each half into a ball. On lightly floured surface, pat each ball into 6-inch round, about ½-inch thick. Cut each round into 16 wedges. On ungreased cookie sheet, arrange wedges about ½ inch apart and with pointed ends toward center. Bake about 15 minutes or until golden brown. Immediately remove from cookie sheet to cooling rack. Cool completely.

3 In small microwavable bowl, place chocolate and shortening. Microwave uncovered on Medium 3 to 4 minutes, stirring after 2 minutes, until mixture can be stirred smooth and is thin enough to drizzle. Drizzle over cookies.

1 Cookie: Calories 95 (Calories from Fat 55); Total Fat 6g (Saturated Fat 3g); Cholesterol 10mg; Sodium 30mg; Total Carbohydrate 9g (Dietary Fiber 0g); Protein 1g

Flavored instant coffees are very popular and come in individual envelopes, boxes of envelopes, cans, canisters and jars. Use your favorite flavor in this recipe.

Hazelnut Biscotti

Prep Time: 25 min ■ Start to Finish: 1 hr 25 min ■ About 40 biscotti

1 cup hazelnuts (filberts), coarsely chopped
1 cup sugar
$^1/_2$ cup butter or margarine, softened
1 teaspoon almond extract
1 teaspoon vanilla
2 eggs
$3^1/_2$ cups all-purpose flour
1 teaspoon baking powder
$^1/_2$ teaspoon baking soda

1 Heat oven to 350°F. Spread hazelnuts in ungreased shallow pan. Bake uncovered about 10 minutes, stirring occasionally, until golden brown; cool.

2 In large bowl, beat sugar, butter, almond extract, vanilla and eggs with electric mixer on medium speed, or mix with spoon. Stir in flour, baking powder and baking soda. Stir in hazelnuts. Place dough on lightly floured surface. Gently knead 2 to 3 minutes or until dough holds together and hazelnuts are evenly distributed.

3 Divide dough in half. On one side of ungreased cookie sheet, shape half of dough into 10 × 3-inch rectangle, rounding edges slightly. Repeat with remaining dough on same cookie sheet.

4 Bake about 25 minutes or until center is firm to the touch. Cool on cookie sheet 15 minutes; move to cutting board. Cut each rectangle crosswise into ½-inch slices, using sharp knife.

5 Place 20 slices, cut sides down, on ungreased cookie sheet. Bake about 15 minutes longer or until crisp and light brown. Immediately remove from cookie sheet to cooling rack; cool. Cool cookie sheet 5 minutes; repeat with remaining slices.

1 Biscotti: Calories 100 (Calories from Fat 35); Total Fat 4g (Saturated Fat 2g); Cholesterol 15mg; Sodium 45mg; Total Carbohydrate 14g (Dietary Fiber 0g); Protein 2g

Rum-Cashew Biscotti

Prep Time: 25 min ▪ Start to Finish: 2 hr ▪ About 3 dozen biscotti

Biscotti
2/3 cup granulated sugar
1/2 cup vegetable oil
2 teaspoons rum extract
2 eggs
2 1/2 cups all-purpose flour
1 cup unsalted cashew pieces
1 teaspoon baking powder
1/4 teaspoon baking soda
1/4 teaspoon salt

Rum Glaze
1/2 cup powdered sugar
2 teaspoons eggnog or half-and-half
1 teaspoon rum or 1/2 teaspoon rum extract

1 Heat oven to 350°F. In large bowl, beat granulated sugar, oil, 2 teaspoons rum extract and the eggs with spoon. Stir in remaining biscotti ingredients.

2 Turn dough onto lightly floured surface. Knead until smooth. On ungreased cookie sheet, shape half of dough at a time into 10 × 3-inch rectangle.

3 Bake 25 to 30 minutes or until toothpick inserted in center comes out clean. Cool on cookie sheet 15 minutes. Cut crosswise into 1/2-inch slices. Place slices, cut sides down, on cookie sheet.

4 Bake about 15 minutes, turning once, until crisp and light brown. Immediately remove from cookie sheet to cooling rack. Cool completely, about 45 minutes. In small bowl, mix all glaze ingredients with spoon until smooth and thin enough to drizzle. Drizzle glaze over biscotti.

1 Biscotti: Calories 110 (Calories from Fat 45); Total Fat 5g (Saturated Fat 1g); Cholesterol 10mg; Sodium 45mg; Total Carbohydrate 13g (Dietary Fiber 0g); Protein 2g

Almond Biscotti

Prep Time: 25 min ▪ Start to Finish: 1 hr 45 min ▪ About 40 biscotti

1 cup slivered almonds
1 cup sugar
$^1/_2$ cup butter or margarine, softened
1 teaspoon almond extract
1 teaspoon vanilla
2 eggs
$3^1/_2$ cups all-purpose flour
1 teaspoon baking powder
$^1/_2$ teaspoon baking soda

1 Heat oven to 350°F. Spread almonds in ungreased shallow pan. Bake uncovered 6 to 10 minutes, stirring occasionally, until golden brown; cool.

2 In large bowl, beat sugar, butter, almond extract, vanilla and eggs with electric mixer on medium speed, or mix with spoon. Stir in flour, baking powder and baking soda. Stir in almonds. On lightly floured surface, gently knead dough 2 to 3 minutes or until dough holds together and almonds are evenly distributed.

3 Divide dough in half. On one side of ungreased cookie sheet, shape half of dough into 10 × 3-inch rectangle, rounding edges slightly. Repeat with remaining dough on same cookie sheet.

4 Bake about 25 minutes or until center is firm to the touch. Cool on cookie sheet 15 minutes; move to cutting board. Cut each rectangle crosswise into 20 ½-inch slices, using sharp knife.

5 Place 20 slices, cut sides down, on ungreased cookie sheet. Bake about 15 minutes longer or until crisp and light brown. Immediately remove from cookie sheet to cooling rack; cool. Cool cookie sheet 5 minutes; repeat with remaining slices.

1 Biscotti: Calories 100 (Calories from Fat 35); Total Fat 4g (Saturated Fat 2g); Cholesterol 15mg; Sodium 45mg; Total Carbohydrate 14g (Dietary Fiber 1g); Protein 2g

Almond Bonbons

Prep Time: 1 hr 5 min ▪ Start to Finish: 1 hr 35 min ▪ About 3 dozen cookies

Cookies
1½ cups all-purpose flour
½ cup butter or margarine, softened
⅓ cup powdered sugar
2 tablespoons milk
½ teaspoon vanilla
½ package (7- or 8-oz size) almond paste

Almond Glaze
1 cup powdered sugar
½ teaspoon almond extract
4 to 5 teaspoons milk
Decorator sugar crystals, if desired

1 Heat oven to 375°F. In large bowl, beat flour, butter, ⅓ cup powdered sugar, 2 tablespoons milk and the vanilla with electric mixer on medium speed, or mix with spoon. Cut almond paste into ½-inch slices; cut each slice into fourths.

2 Shape 1-inch ball of dough around each piece of almond paste. Gently roll to form ball. On ungreased cookie sheet, place balls about 1 inch apart.

3 Bake 10 to 12 minutes or until set and bottom is golden brown. Remove from cookie sheet to cooling rack. Cool completely, about 30 minutes.

4 In small bowl, mix all glaze ingredients with spoon until smooth. Dip tops of cookies into glaze; sprinkle with sugar crystals.

1 Cookie: Calories 70 (Calories from Fat 30); Total Fat 3.5g (Saturated Fat 1.5g); Cholesterol 5mg; Sodium 20mg; Total Carbohydrate 10g (Dietary Fiber 0g); Protein 0g

Add a winter wonderland touch by tinting the glaze with a few drops of food colors in pastel shades. When set, drizzle with additional white glaze. For gifts, pack small cookies in mini paper baking cups or fluted bonbon cups.

Hidden Treasure Cookies

Holiday Melting Moments

Gingersnaps

Ginger-Cranberry Shortbread Wedges

Ginger–Brown Sugar Cookies

Rolled Sugar Cookies

Christmas Cookie Packages

Magic Window Cookies

Peppermint Swirls

Candy Cane Cookies

Spritz

Cherry-Almond Triangles

Chocolate-Raspberry Triangles

Merry Cherry Fudgies

Peppermint Bonbon Brownies

3
festive treats

Hidden Treasure Cookies

Prep Time: 1 hr 15 min ▪ Start to Finish: 1 hr 45 min ▪ About 4 dozen cookies

½ cup powdered sugar
1 cup butter or margarine, softened
1 teaspoon vanilla
2¼ cups all-purpose flour
½ cup finely chopped nuts
¼ teaspoon salt
12 caramels, each cut into 4 pieces
Additional powdered sugar

1 Heat oven to 400°F. In large bowl, mix ½ cup powdered sugar, the butter and vanilla. Stir in flour, nuts and salt until dough holds together.

2 Mold portion of dough around each piece of caramel to form 1-inch ball. On ungreased cookie sheet, place balls about 1 inch apart.

3 Bake 10 to 12 minutes or until set but not brown. In small bowl, place additional powdered sugar. Roll cookies in powdered sugar while warm. Cool completely on cooling rack, about 30 minutes. Roll in powdered sugar again.

1 Cookie: Calories 90 (Calories from Fat 45); Total Fat 5g (Saturated Fat 2g); Cholesterol 10mg; Sodium 45mg; Total Carbohydrate 10g (Dietary Fiber 0g); Protein 0g

Vary the treasures in your cookies! Instead of caramels, try these enticing ideas: candied cherries, malted milk balls, chocolate-covered raisins and gummy fruit candies.

Holiday Melting Moments

Prep Time: 1 hr 15 min ■ Start to Finish: 2 hr 45 min ■ About 3½ dozen cookies

Cookies

1 cup butter, softened (do not use margarine)
1 egg yolk
1 cup plus 2 tablespoons all-purpose flour
½ cup cornstarch
½ cup powdered sugar
2 tablespoons unsweetened baking cocoa
⅛ teaspoon salt

Vanilla Frosting

1 cup powdered sugar
2 tablespoons butter or margarine, softened
1 teaspoon vanilla
2 to 3 teaspoons milk
2 candy canes, about 6 inches long, finely crushed

1 In large bowl, beat 1 cup butter and egg yolk with electric mixer on medium speed, or mix with spoon. Stir in remaining cookie ingredients. Cover; refrigerate about 1 hour or until firm.

2 Heat oven to 375°F. Shape dough into 1-inch balls. On ungreased cookie sheet, place balls about 2 inches apart.

3 Bake 10 to 12 minutes or until set but not brown. Remove from cookie sheet to cooling rack. Cool completely, about 30 minutes.

4 In small bowl, mix all frosting ingredients except candy canes with spoon until smooth and spreadable. Frost cookies; sprinkle with crushed candy canes.

1 Cookie: Calories 80 (Calories from Fat 45); Total Fat 5g (Saturated Fat 2.5g); Cholesterol 20mg; Sodium 40mg; Total Carbohydrate 9g (Dietary Fiber 0g 5g); Protein 0g

Gingersnaps

Prep Time: 1 hr 15 min ■ Start to Finish: 2 hr 45 min ■ About 4 dozen cookies

1 cup packed brown sugar
$^3/_4$ cup shortening
$^1/_4$ cup molasses
1 egg
$2^1/_4$ cups all-purpose flour
2 teaspoons baking soda
1 teaspoon ground cinnamon
1 teaspoon ground ginger
$^1/_2$ teaspoon ground cloves
$^1/_4$ teaspoon salt
Granulated sugar

1 In large bowl, beat brown sugar, shortening, molasses and egg with electric mixer on medium speed, or mix with spoon. Stir in remaining ingredients except granulated sugar. Cover; refrigerate at least 1 hour.

2 Heat oven to 375°F. Lightly grease cookie sheet with shortening or cooking spray.

3 In small bowl, place granulated sugar. Shape dough by rounded teaspoonfuls into balls; dip tops into granulated sugar. Place balls, sugared sides up, about 3 inches apart on cookie sheet.

4 Bake 9 to 12 minutes or just until set. Remove from cookie sheet to cooling rack. Cool completely, about 30 minutes.

1 Cookie: Calories 80 (Calories from Fat 30); Total Fat 3.5g (Saturated Fat 1g); Cholesterol 0mg; Sodium 70mg; Total Carbohydrate 11g (Dietary Fiber 0g); Protein 0g

Ginger-Cranberry Shortbread Wedges

Prep Time: 10 min ▪ Start to Finish: 40 min ▪ 16 cookies

$^2/_3$ cup butter or margarine, softened
$^1/_3$ cup powdered sugar
3 tablespoons finely chopped crystallized ginger
$1^1/_3$ cups all-purpose flour
$^1/_2$ cup dried cranberries, chopped
2 teaspoons granulated sugar

1 Heat oven to 350°F. In large bowl, mix butter, powdered sugar and ginger with electric mixer on medium speed, or mix with spoon. Stir in flour and cranberries.

2 On ungreased cookie sheet, pat dough into 9-inch round. Sprinkle with granulated sugar.

3 Bake about 20 minutes or until golden brown. Cool 10 minutes on cookie sheet on wire rack. Cut into 16 wedges.

1 Cookie: Calories 135 (Calories from Fat 70); Total Fat 8g (Saturated Fat 5g); Cholesterol 20mg; Sodium 60mg; Total Carbohydrate 16g (Dietary Fiber 1g); Protein 1g

Punch up the flavor! Toss ½ cup peanut butter chips, chocolate chips or a combo of both into the dough.

Ginger–Brown Sugar Cookies

Prep Time: 45 min ■ Start to Finish: 45 min ■ About 3 dozen cookies

1 cup packed brown sugar
$^3/_4$ cup butter or margarine, softened
1 teaspoon vanilla
1 egg
2 cups all-purpose flour
$^1/_2$ teaspoon baking soda
$^1/_2$ teaspoon ground ginger
$^1/_2$ cup finely chopped crystallized ginger
2 tablespoons granulated sugar

1 Heat oven to 375°F. In large bowl, beat brown sugar, butter, vanilla and egg with electric mixer on medium speed, or mix with spoon. Stir in flour, baking soda and gingers.

2 Shape dough by rounded teaspoonfuls into 1-inch balls. On ungreased cookie sheet, place balls about 2 inches apart. Flatten to ½-inch thickness with greased bottom of glass dipped in granulated sugar.

3 Bake 8 to 10 minutes or until edges are set. Remove from cookie sheet to cooling rack. Cool completely.

1 Cookie: Calories 95 (Calories from Fat 35); Total Fat 4g (Saturated Fat 2g); Cholesterol 15mg; Sodium 55mg; Total Carbohydrate 14g (Dietary Fiber 0g); Protein 1g

For a frosty white finish, dip half of each cookie into a thin vanilla glaze or melted white chocolate. Let stand on waxed paper until coating sets.

Rolled Sugar Cookies

Prep Time: 1 hr ■ Start to Finish: 1 hr ■ About 4½ dozen cookies

1 box (1 lb 2.25 oz) white cake mix with pudding in the mix
½ cup shortening
⅓ cup butter or margarine, softened
1 teaspoon vanilla, almond or lemon extract
1 egg
Sugar
1 cup vanilla creamy ready-to-spread frosting (from 1-lb container)
Food colors

1 Heat oven to 375°F. In large bowl, beat half of the cake mix (dry), the shortening, butter, vanilla and egg with electric mixer on medium speed until smooth, or mix with spoon. Stir in remaining cake mix.

2 Divide dough into 4 equal parts. On lightly floured cloth-covered surface and with cloth-covered rolling pin, roll each part ⅛ inch thick. Cut into desired shapes; sprinkle with sugar. On ungreased cookie sheet, place shapes about 2 inches apart.

Paint colors on freshly iced, glazed or frosted cookies, using a fine-tip brush.

3 Bake 5 to 7 minutes or until light brown. Cool 1 minute; remove from cookie sheet to cooling rack. In microwavable bowl, microwave frosting uncovered on High 20 to 30 seconds or until melted; stir. Spread frosting evenly over cookies.

4 Stir together small amounts of water and food color. Paint colors on freshly frosted cookies, using fine-tip brush, then swirl colors with brush or toothpick to create marbled designs. Dry completely before storing.

Swirl colors with a brush or toothpick to create marbled designs.

1 Cookie: Calories 120 (Calories from Fat 55); Total Fat 6g (Saturated Fat 3g); Cholesterol 10mg; Sodium 85mg; Total Carbohydrate 15g (Dietary Fiber 0g); Protein 1g

Christmas Cookie Packages

Prep Time: 10 min ▪ Start to Finish: 2 hr 40 min ▪ About 5 dozen cookies

1¹/₂ cups powdered sugar
1 cup butter or margarine, softened
1 teaspoon vanilla
¹/₂ teaspoon almond extract
1 egg
2¹/₂ cups all-purpose flour
1 teaspoon baking soda
1 teaspoon cream of tartar
Decorating icings (any color from 4.25-oz tubes)
Snowflake or star candy decors, if desired
Edible glitter, if desired

1 In large bowl, mix powdered sugar, butter, vanilla, almond extract and egg with spoon. Stir in flour, baking soda and cream of tartar. Cover; refrigerate about 2 hours or until firm.

2 Heat oven to 375°F. Lightly grease cookie sheet with shortening or cooking spray. Divide dough in half. Roll half of dough at a time on lightly floured surface to ¼-inch thickness. Cut into 2-inch squares. Place on cookie sheet.

3 Bake 7 to 8 minutes or until edges are light brown. Remove from cookie sheet to cooling rack. Cool completely, about 30 minutes.

4 Decorate tops of each cookie package with icings to form ribbon and bow; arrange with candies and sprinkle with glitter.

1 Cookie: Calories 100 (Calories from Fat 40); Total Fat 4.5g (Saturated Fat 2.5g); Cholesterol 10mg; Sodium 45mg; Total Carbohydrate 14g (Dietary Fiber 0g); Protein 0g

If you forget to remove your cookies from the cookie sheets in time and the cookies seem to stick, pop the whole sheet back in the hot oven for a minute or two. The heat should soften the cookies slightly, making them easier to remove.

Magic Window Cookies

Prep Time: 1 hr 55 min ■ Start to Finish: 3 hr 25 min ■ About 6 dozen cookies

> 1 cup sugar
> ³/₄ cup butter or margarine, softened
> 1 teaspoon vanilla
> 2 eggs
> 2¹/₂ cups all-purpose flour
> 1 teaspoon baking powder
> ¹/₄ teaspoon salt
> 4 rolls (about 1 oz each) ring-shaped hard candies or other fruit-flavored
>   hard candies

1 In large bowl, beat sugar, butter, vanilla and eggs with electric mixer on medium speed, or mix with spoon. Stir in flour, baking powder and salt. Cover; refrigerate about 1 hour or until firm.

2 Heat oven to 375°F. Cover cookie sheet with cooking parchment paper or foil. On lightly floured cloth-covered surface, roll one-third of dough at a time ⅛ inch thick. Cut into desired shapes. Place on parchment paper. Cut out designs from cookies using smaller cutters or your own patterns. Place whole or partially crushed pieces of candy in cutouts, depending on size and shape of design, mixing colors as desired. Be sure that you use candy pieces that are the same size in the cutouts so it melts evenly. (To crush candy, place in heavy-duty food-storage plastic bag and tap lightly with rolling pin. Because candy melts easily, leave pieces as large as possible.)

3 Bake 7 to 9 minutes or until cookies are very light brown and candy is melted. If candy has not completely spread within cutout design, immediately spread with toothpick or knife. Cool completely on foil, about 30 minutes. Remove cookies gently to cooling rack.

1 Cookie: Calories 50 (Calories from Fat 20); Total Fat 2g (Saturated Fat 1g); Cholesterol 10mg; Sodium 30mg; Total Carbohydrate 8g (Dietary Fiber 0g); Protein 0g

Use candies that are clear or almost clear, not opaque, so cookies will look like stained glass windows.

Peppermint Swirls

Prep Time: 1 hr 5 min ▪ Start to Finish: 1 hr 5 min ▪ About 4 dozen cookies

1 cup butter or margarine, softened
1/3 cup powdered sugar
1 teaspoon vanilla
2 cups all-purpose flour
1/4 teaspoon peppermint extract
1/4 teaspoon red food color
2 tablespoons granulated sugar

1 Heat oven to 350°F. In large bowl, beat butter, powdered sugar and vanilla with electric mixer on medium speed, or mix with spoon. Stir in flour. Divide dough in half. Stir peppermint extract and food color into 1 half. Divide each color of dough in half.

2 Shape each piece of dough on generously floured surface into 12-inch-long rope. Place 2 ropes, 1 red and 1 white, side by side. Twist ropes. Repeat with remaining 2 pieces of dough.

3 Cut twisted ropes into ½-inch pieces; shape each into ball. On ungreased cookie sheet, place balls about 1 inch apart. Flatten to about ¼-inch thickness with greased bottom of glass dipped in granulated sugar.

4 Bake 7 to 9 minutes or until set. Remove from cookie sheet to cooling rack.

1 Cookie: Calories 60 (Calories from Fat 35); Total Fat 4g (Saturated Fat 2g); Cholesterol 10mg; Sodium 25mg; Total Carbohydrate 5g (Dietary Fiber 0g); Protein 0g

See photo on page 74.

Top to bottom: Peppermint Swirls (page 73),
Peanut Butter–Chocolate Cookies (page 89),
Chocolate Crinkles (page 16), Lemon Cookie Tarts (page 48),
Snickerdoodles (page 90) and Candy Cane Cookies

Candy Cane Cookies

Prep Time: 1 hr 30 min ■ Start to Finish: 6 hr ■ About 4½ dozen cookies

1 cup sugar
1 cup butter or margarine, softened
½ cup milk
1 teaspoon vanilla
1 teaspoon peppermint extract
1 egg
3½ cups all-purpose flour
1 teaspoon baking powder
¼ teaspoon salt
½ teaspoon red food color
2 tablespoons finely crushed hard peppermint candies
2 tablespoons sugar

1 In large bowl, beat 1 cup sugar, the butter, milk, vanilla, peppermint extract and egg with electric mixer on medium speed, or stir with spoon. Stir in flour, baking powder and salt. Divide dough in half. Stir food color into 1 half. Cover; refrigerate at least 4 hours.

2 Heat oven to 375°F. For each candy cane, shape 1 rounded teaspoon dough from each half into 4-inch rope by rolling back and forth on floured surface. Place 1 red and 1 white rope side by side; press together lightly and twist. Place on ungreased cookie sheet; curve top of cookie down to form handle of cane.

3 Bake 9 to 12 minutes or until set and very light brown. In small bowl, mix crushed candies and 2 tablespoons sugar; immediately sprinkle over baked cookies. Immediately remove from cookie sheet to cooling rack. Cool completely, about 30 minutes.

1 Cookie: Calories 80 (Calories from Fat 35); Total Fat 3.5g (Saturated Fat 2g); Cholesterol 15mg; Sodium 45mg; Total Carbohydrate 11g (Dietary Fiber 0g); Protein 1g

Easily chop hard candies by putting them in a resealable food-storage plastic bag and whack them with a meat mallet or rolling pin.

Spritz

Prep Time: 1 hr 50 min ∎ Start to Finish: 2 hr 20 min ∎ About 5 dozen cookies

1 cup butter or margarine, softened
1/2 cup sugar
1 egg
2 1/2 cups all-purpose flour
1/4 teaspoon salt
1/4 teaspoon almond extract or vanilla
Few drops of food color, if desired

1 Heat oven to 400°F. In large bowl, beat butter, sugar and egg with electric mixer on medium speed, or mix with spoon. Stir in remaining ingredients.

2 Place dough in cookie press. On ungreased cookie sheet, form desired shapes.

3 Bake 5 to 8 minutes or until set but not brown. Immediately remove from cookie sheet to cooling rack. Cool completely, about 30 minutes.

1 Cookie: Calories 50 (Calories from Fat 30); Total Fat 3g (Saturated Fat 1.5g); Cholesterol 10mg; Sodium 30mg; Total Carbohydrate 6g (Dietary Fiber 0g); Protein 0g

Chocolate Spritz: Stir 2 oz unsweetened baking chocolate, melted and cooled, into butter-sugar mixture. Omit food color.

Spicy Spritz: Stir in 1 teaspoon ground cinnamon, 1/2 teaspoon ground nutmeg and 1/4 teaspoon ground allspice with the flour.

Cherry-Almond Triangles

Prep Time: 25 min ■ Start to Finish: 1 hr 40 min ■ About 24 triangles

Triangles

1 jar (10 oz) maraschino cherries

1 cup all-purpose flour

$1/2$ cup butter or margarine, softened

$1/4$ cup powdered sugar

2 eggs

1 cup sliced almonds

$1/2$ cup granulated sugar

$1/4$ cup all-purpose flour

$1/2$ teaspoon baking powder

Cherry-Almond Glaze

$1/2$ cup powdered sugar

$1/4$ teaspoon almond extract

2 to 3 teaspoons maraschino
cherry juice

1 Heat oven to 350°F. Drain cherries, reserving juice for glaze. Chop cherries; set aside.

2 In small bowl, mix 1 cup flour, the butter and ¼ cup powdered sugar with spoon. Press in bottom of ungreased 9-inch square pan. Bake about 10 minutes or until set.

3 In medium bowl, beat eggs with fork. Stir in cherries and remaining bar ingredients. Spread over baked layer. Bake 20 to 25 minutes longer or until golden brown. Cool completely, about 45 minutes.

4 In small bowl, mix all glaze ingredients with spoon until smooth and thin enough to drizzle. Drizzle over bars. Cut into 6 rows by 2 rows, then cut each bar diagonally in half to form triangles.

1 Triangle: Calories 140 (Calories from Fat 60); Total Fat 7g (Saturated Fat 2.5g); Cholesterol 30mg; Sodium 40mg; Total Carbohydrate 17g (Dietary Fiber 0g); Protein 2g

See photo on page 116.

Chocolate-Raspberry Triangles

Prep Time: 30 min ▪ Start to Finish: 1 hr 50 min ▪ 48 triangles

1¹/₂ cups all-purpose flour

³/₄ cup sugar

³/₄ cup butter or margarine, softened

1 package (10 oz) frozen raspberries in syrup, thawed and drained

¹/₄ cup orange juice

1 tablespoon cornstarch

³/₄ cup miniature semisweet chocolate chips

1 Heat oven to 350°F. In small bowl, mix flour, sugar and butter until crumbly. In bottom of ungreased 13 × 9-inch pan, press dough evenly. Bake 15 minutes.

2 Meanwhile, in 1-quart saucepan, mix raspberries, orange juice and cornstarch. Heat to boiling, stirring constantly. Boil and stir 1 minute. Cool 10 minutes. Sprinkle chocolate chips over crust. Carefully spread raspberry mixture over chocolate chips.

3 Bake about 20 minutes longer or until raspberry mixture is set. Refrigerate about 1 hour or until chocolate is firm. For triangles, cut into 4 rows by 3 rows, then cut each square into 4 triangles.

1 Triangle: Calories 80 (Calories from Fat 35); Total Fat 4g (Saturated Fat 2g); Cholesterol 10mg; Sodium 20mg; Carbohydrate 10g (Dietary Fiber 1g); Protein 1g

Merry Cherry Fudgies

Prep Time: 1 hr 20 min ▪ Start to Finish: 2 hr 20 min ▪ About 2 dozen cookies

Cookies
¼ cup butter or margarine, softened
1 package (3 oz) cream cheese, softened
¾ cup all-purpose flour
¼ cup powdered sugar
2 tablespoons unsweetened baking cocoa
½ teaspoon vanilla

Cherry Fudge Filling
⅔ cup granulated sugar
⅓ cup unsweetened baking cocoa
¼ cup finely chopped red or green
     maraschino cherries, well drained
2 tablespoons butter or margarine,
     softened
1 egg

Cherry Glaze
½ cup powdered sugar
1 to 2 teaspoons red or green
     maraschino cherry juice
Additional red or green maraschino
     cherries, well drained and finely
     chopped, if desired

1 Heat oven to 350°F. In large bowl, beat ¼ cup butter and the cream cheese with electric mixer on medium speed, or mix with spoon. Stir in flour, ¼ cup powdered sugar, 2 tablespoons cocoa and the vanilla.

2 In each of 24 mini muffin cups place mini foil or paper baking cup, if desired. Divide dough into 24 equal pieces. Press each piece in bottom and up side of muffin cup. In small bowl, mix all filling ingredients. Spoon about 2 teaspoons filling into each cup.

3 Bake 18 to 20 minutes or until almost no indentation remains when filling is touched lightly. Cool 1 hour; loosen from cups with tip of knife. Remove from pan to cooling rack. In small bowl, mix ½ cup powdered sugar and the cherry juice until smooth and spreadable. Drizzle glaze over cookies; sprinkle with additional chopped cherries.

1 Cookie: Calories 100 (Calories from Fat 40); Total Fat 4.5g (Saturated Fat 2.5g); Cholesterol 20mg; Sodium 35mg; Total Carbohydrate 14g (Dietary Fiber 0g); Protein 1g

Peppermint Bonbon Brownies

Prep Time: 35 min ▪ Start to Finish: 3 hr 25 min ▪ About 48 brownies

Brownies
4 oz unsweetened baking chocolate
1 cup butter or margarine
2 cups granulated sugar
2 teaspoons vanilla
4 eggs
1$\frac{1}{2}$ cups all-purpose flour
$\frac{1}{2}$ teaspoon salt

Peppermint Cream Cheese Filling
2 packages (8 oz each) cream cheese, softened
$\frac{1}{2}$ cup granulated sugar

2 teaspoons peppermint extract
1 egg
8 drops green food color
$\frac{1}{2}$ cup miniature semisweet chocolate chips

Chocolate Frosting
2 tablespoons butter or margarine
2 tablespoons corn syrup
2 tablespoons water
2 oz unsweetened baking chocolate
$\frac{3}{4}$ to 1 cup powdered sugar

1 Heat oven to 350°F. Grease bottom only of 13 × 9-inch pan with shortening or cooking spray. In 1-quart saucepan, melt 4 oz chocolate and 1 cup butter over low heat, stirring frequently, until smooth; remove from heat. Cool 5 minutes.

2 Meanwhile, beat all filling ingredients except chocolate chips with spoon until smooth. Stir in chocolate chips; set aside.

3 In large bowl, beat chocolate mixture, 2 cups granulated sugar, the vanilla and 4 eggs with electric mixer on medium speed 1 minute, scraping bowl occasionally. Beat in flour and salt on low speed 30 seconds, scraping bowl occasionally. Beat on medium speed 1 minute.

4 Spread half of batter (about 2½ cups) in pan. Spread filling over batter. Carefully spread remaining batter over filling. Gently swirl through batters with knife for marbled design.

5 Bake 45 to 50 minutes or until toothpick inserted in center comes out almost clean. Cool completely, about 2 hours.

6 In 1-quart saucepan, heat 2 tablespoons butter, the corn syrup and water to boiling; remove from heat. Add 2 oz chocolate, stirring until melted. Stir in enough powdered sugar until frosting is spreadable. Spread over brownies. For brownies, cut into 8 rows by 6 rows. Store covered in refrigerator.

1 Brownie: Calories 180 (Calories from Fat 100); Total Fat 11g (Saturated Fat 6g); Cholesterol 45mg; Sodium 90mg; Total Carbohydrate 18g (Dietary Fiber 0g); Protein 2g

family favorites

Gingerbread Cookies

Prep Time: 1 hr 5 min ■ Start to Finish: 3 hr 35 min ■ About 2½ dozen cookies

Cookies
1 cup packed brown sugar
⅓ cup shortening
1½ cups full-flavor molasses
⅔ cup cold water
7 cups all-purpose flour
2 teaspoons baking soda
2 teaspoons ground ginger
1 teaspoon ground allspice

1 teaspoon ground cinnamon
1 teaspoon ground cloves
½ teaspoon salt

Decorator's Frosting, if desired
2 cups powdered sugar
2 tablespoons milk or half-and-half
½ teaspoon vanilla
Food color, if desired

1 In large bowl, beat brown sugar, shortening, molasses and water with electric mixer on medium speed, or mix with spoon. Stir in remaining cookie ingredients. Cover; refrigerate at least 2 hours until firm.

2 Heat oven to 350°F. Lightly grease cookie sheet with shortening or cooking spray. Roll one-fourth of dough at a time ¼ inch thick on floured surface. Cut into desired shapes. Place about 2 inches apart on cookie sheet.

3 Bake 10 to 12 minutes or until no indentation remains when touched. Immediately remove from cookie sheet to cooling rack. Cool completely, about 30 minutes.

4 In small bowl, mix all frosting ingredients with spoon until smooth and spreadable. Decorate cookies with frosting and, if desired, colored sugars and candies.

1 (2½-inch) Cookie: Calories 200 (Calories from Fat 25); Total Fat 2.5g (Saturated Fat 0.5g); Cholesterol 0mg; Sodium 135mg; Total Carbohydrate 42g (Dietary Fiber 0g); Protein 3g

When using cookie cutters that have one wide end and one narrow end, alternate the placement of it as you cut out the cookies. In other words, cut the first cookie with the wide end of the cutter toward you, then cut the next cookie with the narrow end toward you. This way, you can get more cookies out of one batch of dough.

Gingerbread Cookies and
Espresso Thumbprint
Cookies (page 88)

Espresso Thumbprint Cookies

Prep Time: 1 hr 30 min ■ Start to Finish: 1 hr 45 min ■ About 3½ dozen cookies

Cookies
¾ cup sugar
¾ cup butter or margarine, softened
½ teaspoon vanilla
1 egg
1¾ cups all-purpose flour
3 tablespoons unsweetened
  baking cocoa
¼ teaspoon salt

Espresso Filling
¼ cup heavy whipping cream
2 teaspoons instant espresso
  coffee (dry)
1 cup (half 11.5-oz bag) milk
  chocolate chips
1 tablespoon coffee-flavored liqueur,
  if desired
Candy sprinkles or crushed hard
  peppermint candies, if desired

1 Heat oven to 350°F. In large bowl, beat sugar, butter, vanilla and egg with electric mixer on medium speed, or mix with spoon. Stir in flour, cocoa and salt.

2 Shape dough by rounded teaspoonfuls into 1-inch balls. On ungreased cookie sheet, place balls about 2 inches apart. Press thumb or end of wooden spoon into center of each cookie to make indentation, but do not press all the way to cookie sheet.

3 Bake 7 to 11 minutes or until edges are firm. Quickly remake indentations with end of wooden spoon if necessary. Immediately remove from cookie sheet to cooling rack. Cool completely, about 30 minutes.

4 Meanwhile, in 1-quart saucepan, heat whipping cream and coffee over medium heat, stirring occasionally, until steaming and coffee is dissolved. Remove from heat; stir in chocolate chips until melted. Stir in liqueur. Cool about 10 minutes or until thickened. Spoon rounded ½ teaspoon filling into indentation in each cookie. Top with candy sprinkles.

1 Cookie: Calories 90 (Calories from Fat 45); Total Fat 5g (Saturated Fat 2.5g); Cholesterol 15mg; Sodium 40mg; Total Carbohydrate 10g (Dietary Fiber 0g); Protein 1g

See photo on page 87.

Peanut Butter–Chocolate Cookies

Prep Time: 50 min ■ Start to Finish: 50 min ■ About 3 dozen cookies

$\frac{1}{2}$ cup granulated sugar

$\frac{1}{2}$ cup packed brown sugar

$\frac{1}{2}$ cup creamy peanut butter

$\frac{1}{2}$ cup butter or margarine, softened

1 egg

$1\frac{1}{2}$ cups all-purpose flour

$\frac{3}{4}$ teaspoon baking soda

$\frac{1}{2}$ teaspoon baking powder

Additional granulated sugar

About 3 dozen milk chocolate candy drops or pieces

1 Heat oven to 375°F. In large bowl, beat ½ cup granulated sugar, the brown sugar, peanut butter, butter and egg with electric mixer on medium speed, or mix with spoon. Stir in flour, baking soda and baking powder.

2 Shape dough into 1-inch balls. In small bowl, place additional granulated sugar. Roll balls in granulated sugar. Place about 2 inches apart on ungreased cookie sheet.

3 Bake 8 to 10 minutes or until edges are light brown. Immediately press 1 chocolate candy into center of each cookie. Remove from cookie sheet to cooling rack.

1 Cookie: Calories 120 (Calories from Fat 50); Total Fat 6g (Saturated Fat 2.5g); Cholesterol 15mg; Sodium 75mg; Total Carbohydrate 14g (Dietary Fiber 0g); Protein 2g

See photo on page 74.

Snickerdoodles

Prep Time: 50 min ▪ Start to Finish: 50 min ▪ About 4 dozen cookies

1½ cups sugar
½ cup butter or margarine, softened
½ cup shortening
2 eggs
2¾ cups all-purpose flour
2 teaspoons cream of tartar
1 teaspoon baking soda
¼ teaspoon salt
¼ cup sugar
1 tablespoon ground cinnamon

1 Heat oven to 400°F. In large bowl, beat 1½ cups sugar, the butter, shortening and eggs with electric mixer on medium speed, or mix with spoon. Stir in flour, cream of tartar, baking soda and salt.

2 Shape dough into 1¼-inch balls. In small bowl, mix ¼ cup sugar and the cinnamon. Roll balls in cinnamon-sugar mixture. On ungreased cookie sheet, place balls 2 inches apart.

3 Bake 8 to 10 minutes or until set. Immediately remove from cookie sheet to cooling rack.

1 Cookie: Calories 100 (Calories from Fat 40); Total Fat 4.5g (Saturated Fat 1.5g); Cholesterol 15mg; Sodium 55mg; Total Carbohydrate 13g (Dietary Fiber 0g); Protein 1g

Look in the spice section of your supermarket for jars or plastic bottles of sugar-cinnamon mixture—it's ready to go.

See photo on page 74.

Peanut Butter Cookies

Prep Time: 15 min ▪ Start to Finish: 15 min ▪ About 2½ dozen cookies

½ cup granulated sugar
½ cup packed brown sugar
½ cup peanut butter
¼ cup shortening
¼ cup butter or margarine, softened
1 egg
1¼ cups all-purpose flour
¾ teaspoon baking soda
½ teaspoon baking powder
¼ teaspoon salt
Additional granulated sugar

1 Heat oven to 375°F. In large bowl, beat ½ cup granulated sugar, the brown sugar, peanut butter, shortening, butter and egg with electric mixer on medium speed, or mix with spoon. Stir in flour, baking soda, baking powder and salt.

2 Shape dough into 1¼-inch balls. On ungreased cookie sheet, place balls about 3 inches apart. Flatten in crisscross pattern with fork dipped in additional granulated sugar.

3 Bake 9 to 10 minutes or until light brown. Cool 5 minutes; remove from cookie sheet to cooling rack.

1 Cookie: Calories 115 (Calories from Fat 55); Total Fat 6g (Saturated Fat 2g); Cholesterol 10mg; Sodium 95mg; Total Carbohydrate 13g (Dietary Fiber 0g); Protein 2g

Root Beer Float Cookies

Prep Time: 15 min ■ Start to Finish: 1 hr 15 min ■ About 4½ dozen cookies

Cookies

1 cup packed brown sugar

½ cup butter or margarine, softened

2 cups all-purpose flour

⅓ cup finely crushed root beer–
flavored hard candies (about
10 candies)

1 teaspoon baking powder

½ teaspoon baking soda

¼ teaspoon salt

⅛ teaspoon ground cinnamon

⅛ teaspoon ground allspice

2 eggs

Additional finely crushed root beer–
flavored hard candies, if desired

Root Beer Glaze

1 cup powdered sugar

4 to 5 teaspoons root beer or milk

1 Heat oven to 350°F. Grease cookie sheet with shortening or spray with cooking spray. In large bowl, beat brown sugar and butter with electric mixer on medium speed until light and fluffy, or mix with spoon. Stir in remaining cookie ingredients.

2 On cookie sheet, drop dough by rounded teaspoonfuls about 2 inches apart.

3 Bake 8 to 10 minutes or until almost no indentation remains when touched in center and edges are golden brown. Cool 1 minute; remove from cookie sheet to cooling rack. Cool completely, about 20 minutes.

4 Meanwhile, in small bowl, mix glaze ingredients with spoon until smooth and thin enough to drizzle.

5 Drizzle glaze over cookies. Sprinkle with additional candies.

1 Cookie: Calories 65 (Calories from Fat 20); Total Fat 2g (Saturated 1g); Cholesterol 15mg; Sodium 45mg; Total Carbohydrate 11g (Dietary Fiber 0g); Protein 1g

With flavors reminiscent of a soda fountain at an old-time drugstore, these cookies will be a hit with kids and adults alike. Favorite beverages of choice with these unique cookies? Milk or root beer to boost the cookie flavor, or hot chocolate or coffee for a new taste sensation.

Snowy Shovels

Prep Time: 55 min ■ Start to Finish: 55 min ■ 20 cookies

1/2 cup packed brown sugar
1/2 cup butter or margarine, softened
2 tablespoons water
1 teaspoon vanilla
1 1/2 cups all-purpose flour
1/8 teaspoon salt

10 pretzel rods (about 8 1/2 inches long), cut crosswise in half
2/3 cup white vanilla baking chips
2 teaspoons shortening
Miniature marshmallows (about 80 to 100)
White decorator sugar crystals

1 Heat oven to 350°F. In medium bowl, beat brown sugar, butter, water and vanilla with electric mixer on medium speed, or mix with spoon. Stir in flour and salt. Shape dough into twenty 1¼-inch balls.

2 On ungreased cookie sheet, place pretzel rod halves. Press ball of dough onto cut end of each pretzel rod. Press dough to make indentation to look like shovel, but do not press all the way to cookie sheet. Bake about 12 minutes or until set but not brown. Cool 2 minutes. Remove from cookie sheet to cooling rack. Cool completely.

3 Cover cookie sheet with waxed paper. Place shovels on waxed paper. In 1-quart saucepan, melt white vanilla chips and shortening over low heat, stirring occasionally, until smooth; remove from heat. Place 4 or 5 marshmallows in bottom portion of shovel to look like pile of snow. Spoon melted white vanilla over marshmallows and bottom portion of shovel; sprinkle with sugar crystals. If desired, drizzle white vanilla over shovel handle. Let stand until vanilla is firm.

1 Cookie: Calories 190 (Calories from Fat 70); Total Fat 8g (Saturated Fat 5g); Cholesterol 15mg; Sodium 180mg; Total Carbohydrate 27g (Dietary Fiber 0g); Protein 2g

Plan ahead! Cookie dough can be covered and refrigerated up to 24 hours before baking. If it's too firm, let stand at room temperature 30 minutes.

Jolly Santa Cookies

Prep Time: 30 min ■ Start to Finish: 1 hr 20 min ■ About 1½ dozen cookies

½ cup butter or margarine, softened
1 cup granulated sugar
1 teaspoon grated lemon peel
1 egg
2 tablespoons milk
2 cups all-purpose flour
1 teaspoon baking powder
½ teaspoon baking soda
½ teaspoon salt

1 cup plus 2 tablespoons vanilla
　creamy ready-to-spread frosting
　(from 1-lb container)
3 tablespoons red sugar
18 miniature marshmallows
36 currants or semisweet chocolate
　chips
18 red cinnamon candies
¾ cup shredded coconut

1 Heat oven to 400°F. In large bowl, beat butter, granulated sugar and lemon peel with electric mixer on medium speed, or mix with spoon. Stir in egg and milk. Stir in flour, baking powder, baking soda and salt.

2 Onto ungreased cookie sheet, drop dough by rounded tablespoonfuls about 3 inches apart. Press bottom of drinking glass on each until about ¼ inch thick and 3 inches in diameter. Bake 8 to 10 minutes or until light golden brown. Immediately remove from cookie sheet to cooling rack. Cool completely, about 30 minutes.

3 Spread frosting on cookie (frost and decorate each cookie before starting another). Over top third of cookie, sprinkle red sugar for hat; press on miniature marshmallow for tassel. Into center third of cookie, press 2 currants for eyes and 1 cinnamon candy for nose. Over bottom third of cookie, sprinkle coconut for beard.

1 Cookie: Calories 260 (Calories from Fat 90); Total Fat 10g (Saturated Fat 7g); Cholesterol 25mg; Sodium 180mg; Total Carbohydrate 42g (Dietary Fiber 0g); Protein 2g

These absolutely adorable cookies will be enjoyed by "kids" of all ages. Let little hands press on the marshmallows, currants and cinnamon candies.

Christmas Mice Shortbread

Prep Time: 30 min ▪ Start to Finish: 1 hr 30 min ▪ About 15 cookies

15 maraschino cherries with stems, drained
$^2/_3$ cup white vanilla baking chips or chocolate chips
$^1/_2$ teaspoon vegetable oil
1 package (5.3 oz) shortbread triangles
30 sliced almonds
15 white vanilla baking chips or chocolate chips
Shredded coconut, if desired
15 small red candies

1 Cover work surface with piece of waxed paper about 18 inches long. Dry cherries with paper towels.

2 In 6-oz custard cup, microwave $^2/_3$ cup chips and the oil uncovered on High 1 minute to 1 minute 10 seconds or until chips are softened; stir until smooth.

3 Hold 1 cherry by stem (mouse tail), and dip into melted chips, covering completely. Immediately place on shortbread triangle, with tail at 45° angle. Place 2 of the sliced almonds against front of cherry to form mouse ears. Repeat with remaining cherries, shortbread and almonds.

4 Using the remaining melted chips as glue and a toothpick to spread the melted chips, attach the flat side of a whole chip (flat side back) to the base of the almonds to form mouse head. Using melted chips as glue, attach a few shreds of coconut for whiskers and a red candy for nose.

5 Let cool without moving 50 to 60 minutes or until melted chip mixture is firm and completely set. Store in cool place up to 1 week.

1 Cookie: Calories 110 (Calories from Fat 50); Total Fat 5g (Saturated Fat 2.5g); Cholesterol 0mg; Sodium 55mg; Total Carbohydrate 13g (Dietary Fiber 0g); Protein 1g

Double-Frosted Chocolate Sandwich Cookies

Prep Time: 45 min ▪ Start to Finish: 1 hr 15 min ▪ About 3 dozen cookies

1 bag (12 oz) white vanilla baking chips
4 teaspoons shortening
1 package (14 oz) creme-filled chocolate sandwich cookies
1 bag (10 oz) mint-flavored chocolate chips
Decorator sugar crystals, candy decorations, or colored glitter sugars

1 Line cookie sheet with waxed paper. In small microwavable bowl, microwave white baking chips and 2 teaspoons of the shortening uncovered on Medium 4 to 5 minutes or until mixture can be stirred smooth. Dip 18 of the cookies, one at a time, into white chip mixture; place on waxed paper. Refrigerate 5 to 10 minutes or until coating is set.

2 Meanwhile, in small microwavable bowl, microwave mint chocolate chips and remaining 2 teaspoons shortening uncovered on Medium 4 to 5 minutes or until mixture can be stirred smooth. Dip remaining 18 cookies, one at a time, into chocolate mixture; place on waxed paper. Refrigerate 5 to 10 minutes or until coating is set.

3 Drizzle remaining melted chocolate mixture (reheat slightly if mixture has hardened) over tops of white-coated cookies; sprinkle with decorator sugar crystals. Drizzle remaining melted white mixture (reheat slightly if mixture has hardened) over tops of chocolate-coated cookies; sprinkle with decorator sugar crystals. Let stand about 10 minutes or until set.

1 Cookie: Calories 150 (Calories from Fat 70); Total Fat 8g (Saturated Fat 4g); Cholesterol 0mg; Sodium 85mg; Total Carbohydrate 18g (Dietary Fiber 1g); Protein 2g

Minty Middle Treasures

Prep Time: 45 min ▪ Start to Finish: 1 hr 15 min ▪ About 2 dozen cookies

Cookies

¹/₂ cup granulated sugar
¹/₄ cup packed brown sugar
¹/₄ cup shortening
¹/₄ cup butter or margarine, softened
¹/₂ teaspoon vanilla
1 egg
1²/₃ cups all-purpose flour
¹/₂ teaspoon baking soda
¹/₄ teaspoon salt
About 2 dozen foil-wrapped thin
    rectangular chocolate mints,
    unwrapped

Almond Frosting

1 cup powdered sugar
1 tablespoon plus 1 to 2 teaspoons
    milk
¹/₄ teaspoon almond extract or vanilla
Food color, if desired
Candy sprinkles

1 Heat oven to 400°F. In large bowl, beat granulated sugar, brown sugar, shortening, butter, vanilla and egg with electric mixer on medium speed, or mix with spoon. Stir in flour, baking soda, salt.

2 Shape about 1 tablespoon dough around each mint. On ungreased cookie sheet, place cookies about 2 inches apart.

3 Bake 9 to 10 minutes or until light brown. Remove from cookie sheet to cooling rack. Cool completely, about 30 minutes.

4 In small bowl, mix powdered sugar, milk, almond extract and a few drops of food color with spoon until thick enough to coat. Dip tops of cookies into frosting; sprinkle with candy sprinkles.

1 Cookie: Calories 140 (Calories from Fat 50); Total Fat 6g (Saturated Fat 2.5g); Cholesterol 15mg; Sodium 70mg; Total Carbohydrate 21g (Dietary Fiber 0g); Protein 2g

No-Bake Peanut Butter Squares

Prep Time: 20 min ▪ Start to Finish: 50 min ▪ 36 squares

1¹/₂ cups powdered sugar
1 cup graham cracker crumbs (about 12 squares)
¹/₂ cup butter or margarine
¹/₂ cup peanut butter
1 cup white vanilla baking chips or semisweet chocolate chips (6 oz)
Candy decorations, if desired

1 In medium bowl, mix powdered sugar and cracker crumbs. In 1-quart saucepan, heat butter and peanut butter over low heat, stirring occasionally, until melted. Stir into crumb mixture. Press in ungreased 8-inch square pan.

2 In 1-quart saucepan, melt chocolate chips over low heat, stirring frequently. Spread over crumb mixture. Immediately sprinkle with candy decorations. Refrigerate about 30 minutes or until firm.

3 Cut into 6 rows by 6 rows. (To cut diamond shapes, first cut straight parallel lines 1 to 1½ inches apart down the length of the pan. Second, cut diagonal lines 1 to 1½ inches apart across the straight cuts.) Store loosely covered in refrigerator.

1 Square: Calories 100 (Calories from Fat 50); Total Fat 6g (Saturated Fat 2.5g); Cholesterol 5mg; Sodium 45mg; Total Carbohydrate 10g (Dietary Fiber 0g); Protein 1g

Peanut Butter and Jam Bars

Prep Time: 25 min ■ Start to Finish: 45 min ■ 32 bars

Bars

1/2 cup granulated sugar

1/2 cup packed brown sugar

1/2 cup shortening

1/2 cup peanut butter

1 egg

1 1/4 cups all-purpose flour

3/4 teaspoon baking soda

1/2 teaspoon baking powder

1/2 cup red raspberry jam

Vanilla Drizzle

2 tablespoons butter or margarine

1 cup powdered sugar

1 teaspoon vanilla

3 to 4 teaspoons hot water

1 Heat oven to 375°F. In large bowl, beat sugars, shortening, peanut butter and egg with electric mixer on medium speed, or mix with spoon. Stir in flour, baking soda and baking powder.

2 Reserve 1 cup dough. In ungreased 13 × 9-inch pan, press remaining dough. Spread with jam. Crumble reserved dough and sprinkle over jam; gently press into jam. Bake 20 to 25 minutes or until golden brown. Cool completely.

3 In 1-quart saucepan, melt butter over low heat; remove from heat. Stir in powdered sugar and vanilla. Stir in hot water, 1 teaspoon at a time, until smooth and thin enough to drizzle. For bars, cut into 8 rows by 4 rows.

1 Bar: Calories 135 (Calories from Fat 55); Total Fat 6g (Saturated Fat 1g); Cholesterol 5mg; Sodium 70mg; Total Carbohydrate 18g (Dietary Fiber 0g); Protein 2g

Confetti Caramel Bars

Prep Time: 15 min ▪ Start to Finish: 3 hr 5 min ▪ 32 bars

1 cup packed brown sugar
1 cup butter or margarine, softened
1½ teaspoons vanilla
1 egg
2 cups all-purpose flour
½ cup light corn syrup
2 tablespoons butter or margarine
1 cup butterscotch-flavored chips
1½ to 2 cups assorted candies and nuts (such as candy corn,
    candy-coated chocolate candies and salted peanuts)

1 Heat oven to 350°F. In large bowl, beat brown sugar, 1 cup butter, the vanilla and egg with electric mixer on medium speed, or mix with spoon. Stir in flour. Press evenly in bottom of ungreased 13 × 9-inch pan. Bake 20 to 22 minutes or until light brown. Cool 20 minutes.

2 In 1-quart saucepan, heat corn syrup, 2 tablespoons butter and the butterscotch chips over medium heat, stirring occasionally, until chips are melted; remove from heat. Cool 10 minutes.

3 Spread butterscotch mixture over crust. Sprinkle with candies and nuts; gently press into butterscotch mixture. Cover; refrigerate at least 2 hours until butterscotch mixture is firm. For bars, cut into 8 rows by 4 rows.

1 Bar: Calories 200 (Calories from Fat 90); Total Fat 10g (Saturated Fat 5g); Cholesterol 25mg; Sodium 70mg; Total Carbohydrate 26g (Dietary Fiber 0g); Protein 2g

A simple pan of bars can look extraordinary if you cut them into triangles or diamonds, and then place the serving plate on confetti.

See photo on page 116.

Rocky Road Bars

Prep Time: 15 min ▪ Start to Finish: 1 hr 50 min ▪ 24 bars

1 box (1 lb 2.25 oz) chocolate fudge or devil's food cake mix with pudding in the mix
$\frac{1}{2}$ cup butter or margarine, melted
$\frac{1}{3}$ cup water
$\frac{1}{4}$ cup packed brown sugar
2 eggs
1 cup chopped nuts
3 cups miniature marshmallows
$\frac{1}{3}$ cup chocolate creamy ready-to-spread frosting (from 1-lb container)

1 Heat oven to 350°F. Spray bottom and sides of 13 × 9-inch pan with baking spray with flour.

2 In large bowl, mix half of the cake mix, the butter, water, brown sugar and eggs with spoon until smooth. Stir in remaining cake mix and the nuts. Spread in pan.

3 Bake 20 minutes; sprinkle with marshmallows. Bake 10 to 15 minutes longer or until marshmallows are puffed and golden.

4 In small microwavable bowl, microwave frosting uncovered on High 15 seconds; drizzle over bars. Cool completely, about 1 hour. For easier cutting, use plastic knife dipped in hot water. For bars, cut into 6 rows by 4 rows. Store covered.

1 Bar: Calories 205 (Calories from Fat 90); Fat 10g (Saturated Fat 3g); Cholesterol 20mg; Sodium 250mg; Carbohydrate 28g (Dietary Fiber 1g); Protein 2g

Chocolate Spoons

Prep Time: 25 min ▪ Start to Finish: 35 min ▪ About 18 to 24 spoons

1 cup semisweet chocolate chips, white vanilla baking chips or mint-flavored
    chocolate chips (6 oz)
18 to 24 red plastic spoons
Candy decorations, crushed hard peppermint candies, miniature candy-coated
    chocolate chips or decorator sugar crystals, if desired

1 Line cookie sheet with waxed paper. In heavy 1-quart saucepan, melt chocolate chips over lowest possible heat, stirring constantly.

2 Tip saucepan so chocolate runs to one side. Dip bowl portion of each spoon into chocolate. Sprinkle with crushed hard peppermint candies. Place on waxed paper. Let stand about 10 minutes or until chocolate is dry.

3 Wrap spoons in plastic wrap or cellophane.

1 Spoon: Calories 50 (Calories from Fat 25); Total Fat 3g (Saturated Fat 1.5g); Cholesterol 0mg; Sodium 0mg; Total Carbohydrate 6g (Dietary Fiber 0g); Protein 0g

Double-dipping is encouraged for spoons. Dip first into dark chocolate, then after dark chocolate has set, dip into white chocolate, leaving some of the dark chocolate showing. Or, drizzle melted chocolate in a zigzag design over spoons.

See photo on page 108.

Peppermint Wands and
Chocolate Spoons (page 107)

Peppermint Wands

Prep Time: 25 min ▪ Start to Finish: 40 min ▪ 16 wands

$1/_2$ cup semisweet chocolate chips or white vanilla baking chips
2 teaspoons shortening
16 peppermint sticks or candy canes, about 6 inches long
Crushed hard peppermint candies, miniature chocolate chips, candy decorations,
    colored glitter sugars or decorator sugar crystals, if desired

1 Line cookie sheet with waxed paper. In heavy 1-quart saucepan, melt chocolate chips and shortening over lowest possible heat, stirring constantly.

2 Tip saucepan so chocolate runs to one side. Dip 1 peppermint stick at a time into chocolate, coating about one-third to one-half of each stick with chocolate. Place on waxed paper. Let stand about 2 minutes or until chocolate is partially dry.

3 Roll chocolate-dipped ends in crushed peppermint candies. Place on waxed paper. Let stand about 10 minutes or until chocolate is dry. Store loosely covered at room temperature up to 2 weeks.

1 Wand: Calories 90 (Calories from Fat 20); Total Fat 2g (Saturated Fat 1g); Cholesterol 0mg; Sodium 5mg; Total Carbohydrate 18g (Dietary Fiber 0g); Protein 0g

Dip wands first into dark chocolate, then after dark chocolate has set, dip into white chocolate, leaving some of the dark chocolate showing. Or, drizzle melted chocolate in a zigzag design over wands.

Linzer Torte Bars

Lemon-Raspberry Cream Bars

Cream Cheese Brownies

Irish Cream Bars

Brandy Crème Brûlée Bars

Butterscotch Brownies

Toffee Bars

Peanut Butter–Toffee Bars

Cardamom-Cashew Bars

Cashew Brownie Bars

White Chocolate–Macadamia-Caramel Bars

German Chocolate Bars

Chocolate Chip Dream Bars

Triple Chocolate–Cherry Bars

Cinnamon Espresso Bars

Tiramisu Bars

5
decadent bars

Linzer Torte Bars

Prep Time: 10 min ▪ Start to Finish: 1 hr 35 min ▪ 48 bars

1 cup all-purpose flour
1 cup powdered sugar
1 cup ground walnuts
$1/2$ cup butter or margarine, softened
$1/2$ teaspoon ground cinnamon
$2/3$ cup red raspberry preserves

1 Heat oven to 375°F. In large bowl, mix all ingredients except preserves with spoon until crumbly. Press two-thirds of crumbly mixture in ungreased 9-inch square pan. Spread with preserves. Sprinkle with remaining crumbly mixture; press gently into preserves.

2 Bake 20 to 25 minutes or until light golden brown. Cool completely. For bars, cut into 8 rows by 6 rows.

1 Bar: Calories 60 (Calories from Fat 25); Total Fat 3g (Saturated Fat 0g); Cholesterol 0mg; Sodium 25mg; Total Carbohydrate 8g (Dietary Fiber 0g); Protein 0g

Apricot Linzer Bars: Substitute ground almonds for the ground walnuts and apricot preserves for the raspberry preserves.

Lemon-Raspberry Cream Bars

Prep Time: 15 min ▪ Start to Finish: 2 hr 10 min ▪ 48 bars

1 box (1 lb 2.25 oz) lemon cake mix with pudding in the mix
½ cup butter or margarine, softened
2 eggs
¾ cup raspberry preserves
1 package (8 oz) cream cheese, softened
2 tablespoons milk
12 oz white chocolate baking bars, chopped
2 to 3 teaspoons powdered sugar

1 Heat oven 350°F. Grease bottom only of 15 × 10 × 1-inch pan with shortening. In large bowl, mix cake mix, butter and eggs with spoon until well blended. Press evenly in pan with greased or floured fingers.

2 Bake 15 to 20 minutes or until edges are golden brown and crust begins to pull away from sides of pan or toothpick inserted in center comes out clean. Cool 5 minutes. Spread evenly with preserves. Cool 30 minutes.

3 In medium bowl, beat cream cheese and milk with electric mixer on medium speed until smooth; set aside. In 1-quart saucepan, melt white chocolate over low heat, stirring frequently. Add warm melted white chocolate to cream cheese mixture; beat on medium speed until creamy (mixture may look slightly curdled). Carefully spread over preserves.

4 Refrigerate about 1 hour or until set. Sprinkle with powdered sugar. For bars, cut into 8 rows by 6 rows. Store covered in refrigerator.

1 Bar: Calories 140 (Calories from Fat 60); Total Fat 7g (Saturated Fat 4g); Cholesterol 20mg; Sodium 115mg; Total Carbohydrate 17g (Dietary Fiber 0g); Protein 2g

Don't be tempted to use reduced-fat cream cheese (Neufchâtel) instead of regular cream cheese. The white chocolate–cream cheese filling may not get firm enough, even when refrigerated.

Cream Cheese Brownies

Prep Time: 25 min ▪ Start to Finish: 2 hr 50 min ▪ 48 brownies

Cream Cheese Filling

2 packages (8 oz each) cream cheese,
  softened
1/2 cup sugar
2 teaspoons vanilla
1 egg

Brownies

1 cup butter or margarine
4 oz unsweetened baking chocolate
2 cups sugar
2 teaspoons vanilla
4 eggs
1 1/2 cups all-purpose flour
1/2 teaspoon salt
1 cup coarsely chopped nuts

1 Heat oven to 350°F. Grease bottom and sides of 13 × 9-inch pan with shortening.

2 In medium bowl, beat all filling ingredients with electric mixer on medium speed until smooth; set aside.

3 In 1-quart saucepan, melt butter and chocolate over low heat, stirring frequently. Remove from heat; cool 5 minutes.

4 In large bowl, beat chocolate mixture, 2 cups sugar, 2 teaspoons vanilla and 4 eggs with electric mixer on medium speed 1 minute, scraping bowl occasionally. Beat in flour and salt on low speed 30 seconds, scraping bowl occasionally. Beat on medium speed 1 minute. Stir in nuts. Spread 1¾ cups of the batter in pan. Spread filling over batter. Drop remaining batter in mounds randomly over filling; carefully spread to cover cream cheese layer.

5 Bake 45 to 50 minutes or until toothpick inserted in center comes out clean. Cool completely in pan on wire rack, about 2 hours. For brownies, cut into 8 rows by 6 rows. Store covered in refrigerator.

1 Brownie: Calories 165 (Calories from Fat 100); Total Fat11g (Saturate Fat 6g); Cholesterol 45mg; Sodium 85mg; Total Carbohydrates 15g (Dietary Fiber 1g); Protein 2g

Irish Cream Bars

Prep Time: 20 min ▪ Start to Finish: 2 hr 50 min ▪ 24 bars

¾ cup all-purpose flour
½ cup butter or margarine, softened
¼ cup powdered sugar
2 tablespoons unsweetened
    baking cocoa
¾ cup sour cream
½ cup granulated sugar

⅓ cup Irish cream liqueur
1 tablespoon all-purpose flour
1 teaspoon vanilla
1 egg
½ cup heavy whipping cream
Chocolate sprinkles, if desired

1 Heat oven to 350°F. In small bowl, mix ¾ cup flour, the butter, powdered sugar and cocoa with spoon until soft dough forms. Press in bottom of ungreased 8- or 9-inch square pan. Bake 10 minutes.

2 In medium bowl, beat remaining ingredients except whipping cream and chocolate sprinkles with whisk until blended. Pour over baked layer. Bake 15 to 20 minutes longer or until filling is set. Cool slightly; refrigerate at least 2 hours before cutting.

3 For bars, cut into 6 rows by 4 rows. In chilled small bowl, beat whipping cream with electric mixer on high speed until stiff peaks form. Spoon whipped cream into decorating bag fitted with medium writing or star tip. Pipe dollop of cream onto each bar. Top with chocolate sprinkles. Store covered in refrigerator up to 48 hours.

1 Bar: Calories 110 (Calories from Fat 70); Total Fat 7g (Saturated Fat 4g); Cholesterol 35mg; Sodium 35mg; Total Carbohydrate 10g (Dietary Fiber 0g); Protein 1g

Instead of the Irish cream liqueur, substitute ⅓ cup Irish cream nondairy creamer (or ¼ cup half-and-half plus 2 tablespoons cold coffee and 1 teaspoon almond extract).

See photo on page 116.

Clockwise from top left: Cherry-Almond Triangles (page 78),
Confetti Caramel Bars (page 105), Brandy Crème Brûlée and
Irish Cream Bars (page 115)

Brandy Crème Brûlée Bars

Prep Time: 25 min ■ Start to Finish: 1 hr 45 min ■ 36 bars

1 cup all-purpose flour
$^1/_2$ cup sugar
$^1/_2$ cup butter or margarine, softened
5 egg yolks
$^1/_4$ cup sugar
1$^1/_4$ cups heavy whipping cream
1 tablespoon plus 1 teaspoon brandy or 1$^1/_2$ teaspoons brandy extract
$^1/_3$ cup sugar

1 Heat oven to 350°F. In small bowl, mix flour, ½ cup sugar and the butter with spoon. Press on bottom and ½ inch up sides of ungreased 9-inch square pan. Bake 20 minutes.

2 Reduce oven temperature to 300°F. In small bowl, beat egg yolks and ¼ cup sugar with spoon until thick. Gradually stir in whipping cream and brandy. Pour over baked layer.

3 Bake 40 to 50 minutes or until custard is set and knife inserted in center comes out clean. Cool completely, about 30 minutes. For bars, cut into 6 rows by 6 rows. Place bars on cookie sheet lined with waxed paper.

4 In heavy 1-quart saucepan, heat ⅓ cup sugar over medium heat until sugar begins to melt. Stir until sugar is completely dissolved and caramel colored. Cool slightly until caramel has thickened slightly. Drizzle hot caramel over bars. (If caramel begins to harden, return to medium heat and stir until thin enough to drizzle.) After caramel on bars has hardened, cover and refrigerate bars up to 48 hours.

1 Bar: Calories 90 (Calories from Fat 50); Total Fat 6g (Saturated Fat 3g); Cholesterol 45mg; Sodium 20mg; Total Carbohydrate 9g (Dietary Fiber 0g); Protein 0g

Butterscotch Brownies

Prep Time: 15 min ▪ Start to Finish: 45 min ▪ 16 brownies

$\frac{1}{4}$ cup butter or margarine

1 cup packed brown sugar

1 teaspoon vanilla

2 tablespoons milk

1 egg

1 cup all-purpose flour

$\frac{1}{2}$ cup chopped nuts, if desired

1 teaspoon baking powder

$\frac{1}{2}$ teaspoon salt

1 Heat oven to 350°F. Grease bottom and sides of 8-inch square pan with shortening.

2 In 1½-quart saucepan, melt butter over low heat; remove from heat. Stir in brown sugar, vanilla, milk and egg. Stir in remaining ingredients. Spread in pan.

3 Bake about 25 minutes or until golden brown. Cool 5 minutes in pan on wire rack. For brownies, cut into 4 rows by 4 rows while warm.

1 Brownie: Calories 110 (Calories from Fat 25); Total Fat 3g (Saturated Fat 1g); Cholesterol 15mg; Sodium 130mg; Total Carbohydrate 20g (Dietary Fiber 0g); Protein 1g

Toffee Bars

Prep Time: 20 min ▪ Start to Finish: 1 hr ▪ 32 bars

1 cup butter or margarine, softened
1 cup packed brown sugar
1 teaspoon vanilla
1 egg yolk
2 cups all-purpose flour
$1/4$ teaspoon salt
$2/3$ cup milk chocolate chips or 3 bars (1.55 oz each)
    milk chocolate, broken into small pieces
$1/2$ cup chopped nuts

1 Heat oven to 350°F. In large bowl, stir butter, brown sugar, vanilla and egg yolk until well mixed. Stir in flour and salt. Press dough in ungreased 13 × 9-inch pan.

2 Bake 25 to 30 minutes or until very light brown (crust will be soft). Immediately sprinkle chocolate chips over hot crust. Let stand about 5 minutes or until soft; spread evenly. Sprinkle with nuts. Cool 30 minutes in pan on wire rack. For bars, cut into 8 rows by 4 rows while still warm for easiest cutting.

1 Bar: Calories 230 (Calories from Fat 70); Total Fat 8g (Saturated Fat 4g); Cholesterol 25mg; Sodium 65mg; Total Carbohydrate 15g (Dietary Fiber 1g); Protein 1g

Double-Toffee Bars: Stir in ½ cup almond brickle chips with the flour and salt.

Peanut Butter–Toffee Bars

Prep Time: 20 min ■ Start to Finish: 1 hr 50 min ■ 60 bars

1 box (1 lb 2.25 oz) yellow cake mix with pudding in the mix
1 cup crunchy peanut butter
$^1/_2$ cup water
2 eggs
1 bag (10 oz) almond toffee bits or milk
    chocolate toffee bits (1$^3/_4$ cups)
1 package (12 oz) semisweet chocolate
    chips (2 cups)

1 Heat oven to 350°F. Grease bottom and sides of 15 × 10 × 1-inch pan with shortening or spray with cooking spray; lightly flour. In large bowl, mix cake mix, peanut butter, water and eggs with spoon. Stir in toffee bits. Spread evenly in pan.

2 Bake 20 to 25 minutes or until golden brown. Immediately sprinkle chocolate chips over hot bars. Let stand about 5 minutes or until chips are melted; spread evenly. Cool completely. For bars, cut into 10 rows by 6 rows.

1 Bar: Calories 130 (Calories from Fat 65); Total Fat 7g (Saturated Fat 3g); Cholesterol 10mg; Sodium 105mg; Total Carbohydrate 15g (Dietary Fiber 0g); Protein 2g

Cardamom-Cashew Bars

Prep Time: 20 min ▪ Start to Finish: 1 hr 5 min ▪ 48 bars

Crust
1/2 package (8-oz size) reduced-fat
    cream cheese (Neufchâtel)
1/2 cup powdered sugar
1/4 cup packed brown sugar
2 teaspoons vanilla
1 egg yolk
1 1/2 cups all-purpose flour

Filling
1 1/2 cups packed brown sugar
1/2 cup fat-free cholesterol-free egg
    product or 2 eggs

3 tablespoons all-purpose flour
2 teaspoons vanilla
1/2 teaspoon ground cardamom or
    cinnamon
1/4 teaspoon salt
1 1/2 cups cashews, pieces and halves

Orange Drizzle
3/4 cup powdered sugar
1 tablespoon orange juice

1 Heat oven to 350°F. Grease 13 × 9-inch pan. In medium bowl, beat cream
cheese, 1/2 cup powdered sugar and 1/4 cup brown sugar with electric mixer
on medium speed until fluffy. Beat in 2 teaspoons vanilla and the egg yolk.
Gradually stir in 1 1/2 cups flour to make a soft dough. Press dough evenly in pan.
Bake 15 to 20 minutes or until very light brown.

2 In medium bowl, beat all filling ingredients except cashews with electric
mixer on medium speed about 2 minutes or until thick and colored. Stir in
cashews. Spread over baked crust.

3 Bake 19 to 22 minutes longer or until top is golden brown and bars are set
around edges. Cool completely.

4 Mix all drizzle ingredients until smooth and spreadable. Spread evenly over
bars. For bars, cut into 8 rows by 6 rows.

1 Bar: Calories 100 (Calories from Fat 25); Total Fat 3g (Saturated Fat 1g); Cholesterol 10mg; Sodium 55mg;
Total Carbohydrate 16g (Dietary Fiber 0g); Protein 2g

This is the bar to make when you're entertaining friends who are
watching their waistline. These bars are not only low-fat but also rich and
delicious tasting.

Cashew Brownie Bars

Prep time: 15 min ▪ Start to Finish: 1 hr 50 min ▪ 36 bars

Brownies
1 package (15.5 oz) fudge brownie mix

Brown Butter Frosting
$1/4$ cup butter
2 cups confectioners' sugar
2 tablespoons half-and-half
1 teaspon vanilla

Topping
1 oz unsweetened chocolate
1 tablespoon butter
$1/2$ cup chopped cashews

1 Bake Fudgy or Cake-like Brownies as directed on package. Cool.

2 For frosting, in 1-quart saucepan, heat butter over medium heat until delicate brown. Blend in sugar. Beat in half-and-half and vanilla until smooth and of spreading consistency.

3 Spread frosting over bars. Melt chocolate and butter over low heat. When cool, spread over frosting; sprinkle with nuts. When topping is set, cut into 6 rows by 6 rows for bars.

1 Bar: Calories 120 (Calories from Fat 45); Total Fat 5g (Saturated 2g); Cholesterol 5mg; Sodium 65mg; Total Carbohydrate 17g (Dietary Fiber 0g); Protein 2g

Using a brownie mix to start with makes it a snap to cook up these rich, nutty bars at a moment's notice.

White Chocolate–Macadamia–Caramel Bars

Prep Time: 15 min ■ Start to Finish: 2 hr ■ 48 bars

1 box (1 lb 2.25 oz) yellow cake mix with pudding in the mix
1/2 cup vegetable oil
1/4 cup water
2 eggs
1/2 cup butterscotch caramel topping (from 17-oz jar)
1 package (1 lb 2 oz) refrigerated ready-to-bake white chocolate chunk and
    macadamia nut cookies (big variety)

1 Heat oven to 350°F. In large bowl, beat cake mix, oil, water and eggs with electric mixer on low speed until smooth. In ungreased 13 × 9-inch pan, spread batter evenly.

2 Bake 18 to 22 minutes or until top is golden brown. Remove partially baked crust from oven.

3 In 1-cup microwavable measuring cup, microwave caramel topping on High about 15 seconds or until warm and pourable. Lightly drizzle over crust. Crumble cookies over crust.

4 Bake 18 to 23 minutes longer or until golden brown. Cool completely, about 1 hour. For bars, cut into 8 rows by 6 rows.

1 Bar: Calories 130 (Calories from Fat 60); Total Fat 6g (Saturated Fat 2g); Cholesterol 10mg; Sodium 110mg; Total Carbohydrate 17g (Dietary Fiber 0g); Protein 1g

German Chocolate Bars

Prep Time: 15 min ■ Start to Finish: 3 hr 55 min ■ 48 bars

$^2/_3$ cup butter or margarine, softened
1 box (1 lb 2.25 oz) German chocolate cake mix with pudding in the mix
1 container (1 lb) coconut pecan creamy ready-to-spread frosting
1 bag (6 oz) semisweet chocolate chips (1 cup)
$^1/_4$ cup milk

1 Heat oven to 350°F. Lightly grease bottom and sides of 13 × 9-inch pan with shortening. In medium bowl, cut butter into cake mix (dry) using pastry blender or crisscrossing 2 knives, until crumbly. Press half of the mixture (2½ cups) in bottom of pan. Bake 10 minutes.

2 Carefully spread frosting over baked layer; sprinkle evenly with chocolate chips. Stir milk into remaining cake mixture. Drop by teaspoonfuls onto chocolate chips.

3 Bake 25 to 30 minutes or until cake portion is slightly dry to touch. Cool completely, about 1 hour. Cover and refrigerate about 2 hours or until firm. For bars, cut into 8 rows by 6 rows. Store covered in refrigerator.

1 Bar: Calories 135 (Calories from Fat 70); Total Fat 8g (Saturated Fat 4g); Cholesterol 15mg; Sodium 100mg; Total Carbohydrate 15g (Dietary Fiber 0g); Protein 1g

For an easy dessert with restaurant style, place 2 bars on individual serving plates. Top with whipped cream and grated milk chocolate from a candy bar.

Chocolate Chip Dream Bars

Prep Time: 15 min ■ Start to Finish: 2 hr 45 min ■ 32 bars

Bars
1$\frac{1}{2}$ cups packed brown sugar
$\frac{1}{3}$ cup butter or margarine, softened
1 cup all-purpose flour
2 eggs
1 teaspoon vanilla
2 tablespoons all-purpose flour
1 teaspoon baking powder

$\frac{1}{2}$ teaspoon salt
1 bag (6 oz) semisweet chocolate
chips (1 cup)
1 cup milk chocolate chips

Chocolate Glaze
$\frac{3}{4}$ cup milk chocolate chips
2 teaspoons vegetable oil

1 Heat oven to 350°F. In medium bowl, mix ½ cup of the brown sugar and the butter with spoon. Stir in 1 cup flour. In bottom of ungreased 13 × 9-inch pan, press mixture evenly. Bake 10 minutes.

2 In medium bowl, mix eggs, remaining 1 cup brown sugar and the vanilla with spoon. Stir in 2 tablespoons flour, the baking powder and salt. Stir in semisweet and milk chocolate chips. Spread over crust.

3 Bake 15 to 20 minutes or until golden brown. Cool completely in pan on wire rack, about 1 hour. Meanwhile, in 1-quart saucepan, heat glaze ingredients over low heat, stirring constantly, until chocolate is melted. Drizzle bars with glaze. Refrigerate at least 1 hour until firm. For bars, cut into 8 rows by 4 rows. Store at room temperature.

1 Bar: Calories 160 (Calories from Fat 65); Fat 7g (Saturated Fat 4g); Cholesterol 20mg; Sodium 80mg; Total Carbohydrate 22g (Dietary Fiber 1g); Protein 2g

An all-time favorite with a chocolate drizzle, Dream Bars have been popular decade after decade. If you like semisweet chocolate, you can use that instead of the milk chocolate in the glaze. For an easy way to drizzle, pour glaze into a small resealable food-storage plastic bag, seal the bag, snip off a tiny corner, then drizzle away!

Triple Chocolate–Cherry Bars

Prep Time: 15 min ▪ Start to Finish: 2 hr ▪ 48 bars

1 box (1 lb 2.25 oz) chocolate fudge cake mix with pudding in the mix
1 can (21 oz) cherry pie filling
2 eggs, beaten
1 cup miniature semisweet chocolate chips
1 container (1 lb) chocolate creamy ready-to-spread frosting

1 Heat oven to 350°F. Grease bottom and sides of 15 × 10 × 1-inch pan with shortening or spray with cooking spray. In large bowl, mix cake mix, pie filling, eggs and chocolate chips with spoon. Pour into pan.

2 Bake 28 to 38 minutes or until toothpick inserted in center comes out clean. Cool completely, about 1 hour. Spread with frosting. For bars, cut into 8 rows by 6 rows.

1 Bar: Calories 125 (Calories from Fat 35); Total Fat 4g (Saturated Fat 3g); Cholesterol 10mg; Sodium 100mg; Total Carbohydrate 22g (Dietary Fiber 1g); Protein 1g

Triple Chocolate–Strawberry Bars: Substitute strawberry pie filling for the cherry filling.

Cinnamon Espresso Bars

Prep Time: 15 min ▪ Start to Finish: 1 hr 35 min ▪ 48 bars

Bars
1 cup packed brown sugar
$1/3$ cup butter or margarine, softened
1 egg
$1^1/2$ cups all-purpose flour
1 tablespoon instant espresso powder
1 teaspoon baking powder
$1/2$ teaspoon ground cinnamon
$1/4$ teaspoon salt
$1/4$ teaspoon baking soda
$1/2$ cup water

Cinnamon Espresso Glaze
1 cup powdered sugar
$1/4$ teaspoon vanilla
$1/8$ teaspoon ground cinnamon
4 to 5 teaspoons cold espresso coffee
    or strong coffee

1 Heat oven to 350°F. Grease bottom and sides of 13 × 9-inch pan with shortening or spray with cooking spray; coat with flour. In large bowl, beat brown sugar, butter and egg with electric mixer on medium speed until blended, or mix with spoon. Stir in remaining bar ingredients. Spread batter evenly in pan.

2 Bake 20 to 22 minutes or until top springs back when touched in center.

3 Meanwhile, in small bowl, mix all glaze ingredients with spoon until smooth and thin enough to drizzle. Drizzle over bars while warm. Cool completely, about 1 hour. For bars, cut into 8 rows by 6 rows.

1 Bar: Calories 50 (Calories from Fat 15); Total Fat 2g (Saturated Fat 1g); Cholesterol 10mg; Sodium 40mg; Total Carbohydrate 10g (Dietary Fiber 0g); Protein 0g

Espresso gives these bars a rich coffee flavor, but if you don't have it on hand, you could use regular instant coffee granules for a milder flavor.

Tiramisu Bars

Prep Time: 20 min ▪ Start to Finish: 2 hr 20 min ▪ 24 bars

Bars
³/₄ cup all-purpose flour
¹/₂ cup butter or margarine, softened
¹/₄ cup powdered sugar
1 cup granulated sugar
³/₄ cup whipping cream
¹/₄ cup butter or margarine, melted
3 tablespoons all-purpose flour
1 tablespoon instant coffee granules
   or crystals

¹/₂ teaspoon vanilla
2 eggs
3 oz semisweet baking chocolate,
   grated (about 1¹/₄ cups)

Frosting
1 package (3 oz) cream cheese,
   softened
¹/₄ cup whipping cream
Chocolate curls, if desired

1 Heat oven to 350°F. In medium bowl, beat ¾ cup flour, ½ cup softened butter and the powdered sugar with electric mixer on medium speed until soft dough forms. In bottom of ungreased 8-inch square pan, spread dough evenly. Bake 10 minutes.

2 Meanwhile, in medium bowl, beat remaining bar ingredients, except grated chocolate, with whisk until smooth. Set aside.

3 Sprinkle 1 cup of the grated chocolate over hot baked crust. Pour egg mixture over chocolate.

4 Bake 40 to 45 minutes longer or until golden brown and set. Cool completely in pan on wire rack, about 1 hour 15 minutes.

5 In medium bowl, beat cream cheese and ¼ cup whipping cream on medium speed about 2 minutes or until fluffy. Spread evenly over cooled bars. Sprinkle with remaining grated chocolate. For bars, cut into 6 rows by 4 rows. Garnish each with chocolate curl. Store covered in refrigerator.

1 Bar: Calories 180 (Calories from Fat 110); Total Fat 12g (Saturated Fat 8g); Cholesterol 50mg; Sodium 60mg; Total Carbohydrate 15g (Dietary Fiber 0g); Protein 2g

6

scrumptious gifts

Creamy Chocolate Marble Fudge

Prep Time: 40 ■ Start to Finish: 3 hr 40 min ■ About 8 dozen candies

6 cups sugar
1 can (12 oz) evaporated milk
1 cup butter or margarine
1 package (8 oz) cream cheese, softened
2 jars (7 oz each) marshmallow creme or 1 bag (10.5 oz)
    miniature marshmallows
1 tablespoon vanilla
1 bag (12 oz) white vanilla baking chips (2 cups)
1 cup milk chocolate chips (6 oz)
1 cup semisweet chocolate chips (6 oz)
2 tablespoons unsweetened baking cocoa
1/2 cup chopped nuts, if desired

1 Butter bottom and sides of 13 × 9-inch pan or line with foil, leaving 1 inch of foil overhanging at 2 opposite sides of pan. In 6-quart Dutch oven, heat sugar, milk, butter and cream cheese to boiling over medium-high heat; cook 6 to 8 minutes, stirring constantly. Reduce heat to medium. Cook about 10 minutes, stirring occasionally, to 225°F on candy thermometer; remove from heat.

2 Quickly stir in marshmallow creme and vanilla. In large bowl, pour 4 cups hot marshmallow mixture over white baking chips; stir to mix. Into remaining marshmallow mixture, stir milk chocolate chips, semisweet chocolate chips, cocoa and nuts.

3 Pour one-third of the white mixture into pan, spreading evenly. Quickly pour one-third of the chocolate mixture over top, spreading evenly. Repeat twice. Swirl knife greased with butter through mixtures for marbled design. Cool until set.

4 Refrigerate uncovered about 3 hours or until set. Cut into 12 rows by 8 rows with knife greased with butter. Store covered in refrigerator.

1 Candy: Calories 130 (Calories from Fat 45); Total Fat 5g (Saturated Fat 3g); Cholesterol 10mg; Sodium 35mg; Total Carbohydrate 21g (Dietary Fiber 0g); Protein 0g

Deluxe Christmas Fudge

Prep Time: 20 min ▪ Start to Finish: 2 hr 20 min ▪ About 6 dozen candies

1½ bags (12-oz size) semisweet chocolate chips (3 cups)
2 cups miniature marshmallows or 16 large marshmallows, cut in half
1 can (14 oz) sweetened condensed milk
1 teaspoon vanilla
1 cup pistachio nuts
½ cup chopped candied cherries
¼ cup white vanilla baking chips, melted, if desired

1 Line 9-inch square pan with foil, leaving 1 inch of foil overhanging at 2 opposite sides of pan. Grease foil with butter.

2 In 8-cup microwavable measuring cup, place chocolate chips, marshmallows and milk. Microwave uncovered on High 3 to 5 minutes, stirring every minute, until marshmallows and chips are melted and can be stirred smooth.

3 Stir in vanilla, nuts and cherries. Immediately pour into pan. Drizzle with melted white baking chips. Refrigerate about 2 hours or until firm. Remove fudge from pan, using foil edges to lift. Cut into 9 rows by 8 rows, or cut into diamond shapes.

1 Candy: Calories 80 (Calories from Fat 30); Total Fat 3.5g (Saturated Fat 1.5g); Cholesterol 0mg; Sodium 10mg; Total Carbohydrate 10g (Dietary Fiber 0g); Protein 1g

Hazelnut Fudge: Omit cherries; substitute hazelnuts for the pistachios and add 2 tablespoons hazelnut liqueur.

Toffee

Prep Time: 35 min ■ Start to Finish: 1 hr 35 min ■ About 3 dozen candies

1 cup sugar
1 cup butter or margarine
¼ cup water
½ cup semisweet chocolate chips
½ cup finely chopped pecans

1 In heavy 2-quart saucepan, heat sugar, butter and water to boiling, stirring constantly; reduce heat to medium. Cook about 13 minutes, stirring constantly, to 300°F on candy thermometer or until small amount of mixture dropped into cup of very cold water separates into hard, brittle threads. (Watch carefully so mixture does not burn.)

2 Immediately pour toffee onto ungreased large cookie sheet. If necessary, quickly spread mixture to ¼-inch thickness. Sprinkle with chocolate chips; let stand about 1 minute or until chips are completely softened. Spread softened chocolate evenly over toffee. Sprinkle with pecans.

3 Let stand at room temperature about 1 hour, or refrigerate if desired, until firm. Break into bite-size pieces. Store in airtight container.

1 Candy: Calories 90 (Calories from Fat 60); Total Fat 7g (Saturated Fat 3g); Cholesterol 15mg; Sodium 35mg; Total Carbohydrate 7g (Dietary Fiber 0g); Protein 0g

See photo on page 138.

Maple-Nut Brittle and
Toffee (page 137)

Maple-Nut Brittle

Prep Time: 30 min ■ Start to Finish: 1 hr 30 min ■ About 3 dozen candies

1 cup packed brown sugar
1/2 cup maple-flavored syrup
1 can (about 12 oz) lightly salted mixed nuts (2 cups)
1 tablespoon butter or margarine
1 teaspoon baking soda

1 Heat oven to 200°F. Generously butter large cookie sheet; keep warm in oven.

2 In 8-cup microwavable measure, mix brown sugar and maple syrup. Microwave uncovered on High 5 minutes.

3 Stir in nuts. Microwave uncovered on High 5 to 7 minutes or until syrup is bubbling and nuts are toasted—syrup will be very hot.

4 Stir in butter. Microwave uncovered on High 1 minute. Quickly and thoroughly stir in baking soda until mixture is light and foamy. Pour onto cookie sheet; quickly spread candy.

5 Cool 30 to 60 minutes or until hardened. Break into pieces. Store candy in airtight container at room temperature up to 2 weeks.

1 Candy: Calories 90 (Calories from Fat 45); Total Fat 5g (Saturated Fat 1g); Cholesterol 0mg; Sodium 60mg; Total Carbohydrate 11g (Dietary Fiber 0g); Protein 1g;

Caramels

Prep Time: 45 min ▪ Start to Finish: 2 hr 45 min ▪ About 64 candies

2 cups sugar
1/2 cup butter or margarine
2 cups heavy whipping cream
3/4 cup light corn syrup

1 Butter bottom and sides of 8- or 9-inch square glass baking dish.

2 In heavy 3-quart saucepan, heat all ingredients to boiling over medium heat, stirring constantly. Boil uncovered about 35 minutes, stirring frequently, to 245°F on candy thermometer or until small amount of mixture dropped into cup of very cold water forms a firm ball that holds its shape until pressed. Immediately spread in baking dish. Cool completely, about 2 hours.

3 Cut into 1-inch squares. Wrap individually in waxed paper or plastic wrap. Store wrapped candies in airtight container.

1 Candy: Calories 80 (Calories from Fat 40); Total Fat 4g (Saturated Fat 2.5g); Cholesterol 15mg; Sodium 15mg; Total Carbohydrate 9g (Dietary Fiber 0g); Protein 0g

Chocolate Caramels: Heat 2 oz unsweetened baking chocolate with the sugar mixture.

Pralines

Prep Time: 15 min ▪ Start to Finish: 3 hr ▪ About 18 candies

2 cups packed light brown sugar
1 cup granulated sugar
1¼ cups milk
¼ cup light corn syrup
⅛ teaspoon salt
1 teaspoon vanilla
1½ cups pecan halves (5½ oz)

1 In heavy 3-quart saucepan, heat sugars, milk, corn syrup and salt to boiling, stirring constantly. Reduce heat to medium. Cook uncovered about 15 minutes, without stirring, to 236°F on candy thermometer or until small amount of mixture dropped into cup of very cold water forms a soft ball that flattens when removed from water. Cool about 1 hour, without stirring, until saucepan is cool to the touch.

2 Add vanilla and pecan halves. Beat with spoon about 1 minute or until mixture is slightly thickened and just coats pecans but does not lose its gloss. On waxed paper, drop mixture by spoonfuls, dividing pecans equally. Let stand uncovered 1 to 2 hours or until candies are firm and no longer glossy.

3 Wrap candies individually in waxed paper or plastic wrap. Store in airtight container.

1 Candy: Calories. 230 (Calories from Fat 65); Total Fat 7g (Saturated Fat 1g); Cholesterol 0mg; Sodium 40mg; Total Carbohydrate 40g (Dietary Fiber 1g); Protein 1g

Divinity

Prep Time: 55 min ▪ Start to Finish: 4 hr 55 min ▪ About 4 dozen candies

2²/₃ cups sugar
²/₃ cup light corn syrup
¹/₂ cup water
2 egg whites
1 teaspoon vanilla
²/₃ cup coarsely chopped nuts

1 Line cookie sheet with waxed paper. In 2-quart saucepan, cook sugar, corn syrup and water (use 1 tablespoon less water on humid days) over low heat, stirring constantly, until sugar is dissolved. Cook without stirring to 260°F on candy thermometer or until small amount of mixture dropped into cup of very cold water forms a hard ball that holds its shape but is pliable.

2 In medium bowl, beat egg whites with electric mixer on high speed until stiff peaks form. (For best results, use electric stand mixer, not a portable handheld mixer, because total beating time is about 6 minutes and mixture is thick.) Continue beating on medium speed while pouring hot syrup in a thin stream into egg whites. Add vanilla. Beat until mixture holds its shape and becomes slightly dull. (If mixture becomes too stiff for mixer, continue beating with wooden spoon.) Fold in nuts.

3 Quickly drop mixture from buttered spoon onto waxed paper. Let stand at room temperature at least 4 hours, but no longer than 12 hours, until candies feel firm and dry to the touch. Store in airtight container at room temperature.

1 Candy: Calories 70 (Calories from Fat 10); Total Fat 1g (Saturated Fat 0g); Cholesterol 0mg; Sodium 10mg; Total Carbohydrate 15g (Dietary Fiber 0g); Protein 0g

Peanut Brittle

Prep Time: 15 min ▪ Start to Finish: 1 hr ▪ About 6 dozen candies

1½ teaspoons baking soda
1 teaspoon water
1 teaspoon vanilla
1½ cups sugar
1 cup water
1 cup light corn syrup
3 tablespoons butter or margarine
1 lb unsalted raw Spanish peanuts (3 cups)

1 Heat oven to 200°F. Grease 2 cookie sheets with butter; keep warm in oven. (Keeping the cookie sheets warm allows the candy to be spread ¼ inch thick without it setting up.) Grease long metal spatula with butter; set aside.

2 In small bowl, mix baking soda, 1 teaspoon water and the vanilla; set aside. In 3-quart saucepan, mix sugar, 1 cup water and the corn syrup. Cook over medium heat about 25 minutes, stirring occasionally, to 240°F on candy thermometer or until small amount of mixture dropped into cup of very cold water forms a soft ball that flattens when removed from water.

3 Stir in butter and peanuts. Cook over medium heat about 13 minutes, stirring constantly, to 300°F or until small amount of mixture dropped into cup of very cold water separates into hard, brittle threads. (Watch carefully so mixture does not burn.) Immediately remove from heat. Quickly stir in baking soda mixture until light and foamy.

4 Pour half of the candy mixture onto each cookie sheet and quickly spread about ¼ inch thick with buttered spatula. Cool completely, at least 1 hour. Break into pieces. Store in airtight container up to 2 weeks.

1 Candy: Calories. 80 (Calories from Fat 35); Total Fat 4g (Saturated Fat 1g); Cholesterol 0mg; Sodium 35mg; Total Carbohydrates 9g (Dietary Fiber 0g); Protein 2g

Peppermint Bark

Prep Time: 15 min ▪ Start to Finish: 1 hr 15 min ▪ About 16 candies

1 package (16 oz) vanilla-flavored candy
   coating (almond bark), broken into pieces
24 hard peppermint candies

1 Line cookie sheet with waxed paper, foil or cooking parchment paper. In 8-cup microwavable measure or 2-quart microwavable casserole, place candy coating. Microwave uncovered on High 2 to 3 minutes, stirring every 30 seconds, until almost melted. Stir until smooth.

2 Place peppermint candies in heavy food-storage plastic bag; crush with rolling pin or bottom of small heavy-duty saucepan. Pour crushed candies into strainer. Shake strainer over melted coating until all of the tiniest candy pieces fall into coating; reserve larger candy pieces. Stir coating to mix evenly.

3 Spread coating evenly on waxed paper. Sprinkle evenly with reserved candy pieces. Let stand about 1 hour or until cool and hardened. Break into pieces.

1 Candy: Calories 190 (Calories from Fat 80); Total Fat 9g (Saturated Fat 6g); Cholesterol 0mg; Sodium 30mg; Total Carbohydrate 24g (Dietary Fiber 0g); Protein 2g

Rum Balls

Prep Time: 20 min ▪ Start to Finish: 5 days 20 min ▪ About 5 dozen candies

1 package (9 oz) thin chocolate wafer cookies,
    finely crushed (about 2 cups)
2 cups finely chopped almonds, pecans or walnuts
2½ cups powdered sugar
¼ cup light rum
¼ cup light corn syrup

1 In large bowl, mix cookies, almonds and 2 cups of the powdered sugar. Stir in rum and corn syrup. Shape mixture into 1-inch balls.

2 In small bowl, place remaining ½ cup powdered sugar. Roll balls in sugar. Cover tightly and refrigerate at least 5 days before serving to blend flavors.

1 Candy: Calories 70 (Calories from Fat 25); Total Fat 3g (Saturated Fat 0g); Cholesterol 0mg; Sodium 25mg; Total Carbohydrate 10g (Dietary Fiber 0g); Protein 1g

For a clever, amusing way to show off these favorites, place individual balls in shot glasses—or put more in champagne or martini glasses.

Decadent Fudge Sauce

Prep Time: 10 min ▪ Start to Finish: 10 min ▪ About 3 cups sauce

> 1 can (12 oz) evaporated milk
> 1 bag (12 oz) semisweet chocolate chips (2 cups)
> 1/2 cup sugar
> 1 tablespoon butter or margarine
> 2 teaspoons orange-flavored liqueur or 1 teaspoon orange extract, if desired

1 In 2-quart saucepan, heat milk, chocolate chips and sugar to boiling over medium heat, stirring constantly; remove from heat.

2 Stir in butter and liqueur until sauce is smooth and creamy. Serve warm. Store covered in refrigerator up to 4 weeks. Reheat slightly before serving if desired.

1 Serving (1 tablespoon sauce): Calories 60 (Calories from Fat 25); Total Fat 2.5g (Saturated Fat 1.5g); Cholesterol 0mg; Sodium 10mg; Total Carbohydrate 7g (Dietary Fiber 0g); Protein 0g

Classic Fudge Sauce: Omit the liqueur and add 1 teaspoon vanilla.

Irish Cream Fudge Sauce: Substitute 2 tablespoons Irish cream liqueur for the orange liqueur.

Raspberry–Chocolate Fudge Sauce: Substitute 2 tablespoons raspberry-flavored liqueur for the orange liqueur.

Divine Caramel Sauce

Prep Time: 15 min ▪ Start to Finish: 45 min ▪ About 2 1/2 cups sauce

1 cup light corn syrup
1 1/4 cups packed brown sugar
1/4 cup butter or margarine
1 cup heavy whipping cream

1 In 2-quart saucepan, heat corn syrup, brown sugar and butter to boiling over low heat, stirring constantly. Boil 5 minutes, stirring occasionally.

2 Stir in whipping cream; heat to boiling. Cool about 30 minutes. Serve warm. Store covered in refrigerator up to 2 months. Reheat slightly before serving if desired.

1 Serving (1 tablespoon sauce): Calories 80 (Calories from Fat 30); Total Fat 3.5g (Saturated Fat 2g); Cholesterol 10mg; Sodium 25mg; Total Carbohydrate 13g (Dietary Fiber 0g); Protein 0g

Divine Toasted Pecan–Caramel Sauce: Add 1 cup chopped toasted pecans after cooling in step 2.

Mixed-Berry Jam

Prep Time: 25 min ▪ Start to Finish: 24 hr 25 min ▪ About 5 half-pints jam

1 cup crushed strawberries (1 pint whole berries)
1 cup crushed raspberries (1 pint whole berries)
4 cups sugar
½ teaspoon grated lemon peel
1 tablespoon lemon juice
1 pouch (3 oz) liquid fruit pectin

1 In large glass or plastic bowl, mix berries and sugar. Let stand at room temperature about 10 minutes, stirring occasionally, until sugar is dissolved.

2 Stir in lemon peel, lemon juice and pectin. Stir 3 to 5 minutes or until slightly thickened.

3 Spoon mixture into freezer containers, leaving ½-inch headspace. Seal immediately. Let stand at room temperature until set, about 24 hours. Refrigerate up to 3 weeks, or freeze up to 1 year (thaw in refrigerator or at room temperature before serving). Use as a spread or in desserts.

1 Serving (1 tablespoon jam): Calories 45 (Calories from Fat 0); Total Fat 0g (Saturated Fat 0g); Cholesterol 0mg; Sodium 0mg; Total Carbohydrate 11g (Dietary Fiber 0g); Protein 0g

If fresh berries aren't available, frozen berries, thawed and drained, are a good substitute.

Lemon Curd

Prep Time: 25 min ▪ Start to Finish: 25 min ▪ About 2 cups curd

1 cup sugar
1 tablespoon finely shredded lemon peel
1 cup lemon juice (5 large lemons)
3 tablespoons firm butter or margarine, cut up
3 eggs, slightly beaten

1 In heavy 1½-quart saucepan, mix sugar, lemon peel and lemon juice with whisk.

2 Stir in butter and eggs. Cook over medium heat about 8 minutes, stirring constantly, until mixture thickens and coats back of spoon (do not boil). Immediately pour into one 1-pint container or two 1-cup containers.

3 Store covered in refrigerator up to 2 months.

1 Serving (1 tablespoon curd): Calories 45 (Calories from Fat 15); Total Fat 1.5g (Saturated Fat 0.5g; Trans Fat 0g); Cholesterol 25mg; Sodium 15mg; Total Carbohydrate 7g (Dietary Fiber 0g; Sugars 6g); Protein 0g

Key Lime Curd: Substitute lime peel for the lemon peel and Key lime juice for the lemon juice.

Easy Festive Peppermint Marshmallows

Prep Time: 15 min ▪ Start to Finish: 8 hr 15 min ▪ About 40 marshmallows

Powdered sugar
2$\frac{1}{2}$ tablespoons unflavored gelatin
$\frac{1}{2}$ cup cold water
1$\frac{1}{2}$ cups granulated sugar

1 cup corn syrup
$\frac{1}{4}$ teaspoon salt
$\frac{1}{2}$ cup water
1 teaspoon peppermint extract

1 Generously dust 11 × 7-inch glass baking dish with powdered sugar. In large bowl, sprinkle gelatin on $\frac{1}{2}$ cup cold water to soften; set aside.

2 In 2-quart saucepan, heat granulated sugar, corn syrup, salt and $\frac{1}{2}$ cup water over low heat, stirring constantly, until sugar is dissolved. Heat to boiling; cook without stirring to 250°F on candy thermometer or until small amount of mixture dropped into cup of very cold water forms a ball that holds its shape but is pliable; remove from heat.

3 Slowly pour syrup into softened gelatin while beating with electric mixer on high speed. Beat on high speed until mixture is white and has almost tripled in volume. Add peppermint extract; beat on high speed 1 minute. Pour into pan. Sprinkle with powdered sugar, patting lightly with hands. Let stand uncovered at least 8 hours.

4 Place cutting board upside down on dish of marshmallows; turn board and dish over to remove marshmallow mixture. Cut into shapes with miniature cookie cutters or knife dipped in water to keep from sticking. Store in airtight container at room temperature up to 3 weeks.

1 Marshmallow: Calories 60 (Calories from Fat 0); Total Fat 0g (Saturated Fat 0g); Cholesterol 0mg; Sodium 25mg; Total Carbohydrate 14g (Dietary Fiber 0g); Protein 0g

These tasty treats make great gifts. Package a collection of them in a plastic bag, and tie with a curly ribbon. Place bags of marshmallows in oversized mugs along with packages of gourmet cocoa.

Luscious Chocolate Truffles

Prep Time: 20 min ■ Start to Finish: 1 hr 25 min ■ About 2 dozen candies

1 bag (12 oz) semisweet chocolate chips (2 cups)
2 tablespoons butter or margarine
1/4 cup heavy whipping cream
2 tablespoons liqueur (almond, cherry, coffee, hazelnut, Irish cream, orange, raspberry, etc.), if desired
1 tablespoon shortening
Finely chopped nuts, if desired
1/4 cup powdered sugar, if desired
1/2 teaspoon milk, if desired

1 Line cookie sheet with foil. In heavy 2-quart saucepan, melt 1 cup of the chocolate chips over low heat, stirring constantly; remove from heat. Stir in butter. Stir in whipping cream and liqueur. Refrigerate 10 to 15 minutes, stirring frequently, just until thick enough to hold a shape.

2 Drop mixture by teaspoonfuls onto foil. Shape into balls. (If mixture is too sticky, refrigerate until firm enough to shape.) Freeze 30 minutes.

3 In 1-quart saucepan, heat shortening and remaining 1 cup chocolate chips over low heat, stirring constantly, until chocolate is melted and mixture is smooth; remove from heat. Using fork, dip truffles, one at a time, into chocolate. Return to foil-covered cookie sheet. Immediately sprinkle some of the truffles with nuts. Refrigerate about 10 minutes or until coating is set.

4 In small bowl, stir powdered sugar and milk until smooth; drizzle over some of the truffles. Refrigerate just until set. Store in airtight container in refrigerator. Serve truffles at room temperature by removing from refrigerator about 30 minutes before serving.

1 Candy: Calories 100 (Calories from Fat 60); Total Fat 7g (Saturated Fat 3.5g); Cholesterol 5mg; Sodium 10mg; Total Carbohydrate 9g (Dietary Fiber 0g); Protein 0g

Helpful Nutrition and Cooking Information

Recommended intake for a daily diet of 2,000 calories as set by the Food and Drug Administration

Total Fat	Less than 65g
Saturated Fat	Less than 20g
Cholesterol	Less than 300mg
Sodium	Less than 2,400mg
Total Carbohydrate	300g
Dietary Fiber	25g

Calculating Nutrition Information

- The first ingredient was used wherever a choice is given (such as 1/3 cup sour cream or plain yogurt).

- The first ingredient amount was used wherever a range is given (such as 3- to 3½-pound cut-up broiler-fryer chicken).

- The first serving number was used wherever a range is given (such as 4 to 6 servings).

- "If desired" ingredients and recipe variations were not included (such as sprinkle with brown sugar, if desired).

- Only the amount of a marinade or frying oil that is estimated to be absorbed by the food during preparation or cooking was calculated.

Ingredients Used in Recipe Testing and Nutrition Calculations

- Ingredients used for testing represent those that the majority of consumers use in their homes: large eggs, 2% milk, 80%-lean ground beef, canned ready-to-use chicken broth and vegetable oil spread containing not less than 65% fat.

- Fat-free, low-fat or low-sodium products were not used, unless otherwise indicated.

- Solid vegetable shortening (not butter, margarine, nonstick cooking sprays or vegetable oil spread as they can cause sticking problems) was used to grease pans, unless otherwise indicated.

Equipment Used in Recipe Testing

We use equipment for testing that the majority of consumers use in their homes. If a specific piece of equipment (such as a whisk) is necessary for recipe success, it is listed in the recipe.

- Cookware and bakeware without nonstick coatings were used, unless otherwise indicated.

- No dark-colored, black or insulated bakeware was used.

- When a pan is specified in a recipe, a metal pan was used; a baking dish or pie plate means ovenproof glass was used.

- An electric hand mixer was used for mixing only when mixer speeds are specified in the recipe directions. When a mixer speed is not given, a spoon or fork was used.

Metric Conversion Guide

VOLUME

U.S. Units	Canadian Metric	Australian Metric
1/4 teaspoon	1 mL	1 ml
1/2 teaspoon	2 mL	2 ml
1 teaspoon	5 mL	5 ml
1 tablespoon	15 mL	20 ml
1/4 cup	50 mL	60 ml
1/3 cup	75 mL	80 ml
1/2 cup	125 mL	125 ml
2/3 cup	150 mL	170 ml
3/4 cup	175 mL	190 ml
1 cup	250 mL	250 ml
1 quart	1 liter	1 liter
1 1/2 quarts	1.5 liters	1.5 liters
2 quarts	2 liters	2 liters
2 1/2 quarts	2.5 liters	2.5 liters
3 quarts	3 liters	3 liters
4 quarts	4 liters	4 liters

WEIGHT

U.S. Units	Canadian Metric	Australian Metric
1 ounce	30 grams	30 grams
2 ounces	55 grams	60 grams
3 ounces	85 grams	90 grams
4 ounces (1/4 pound)	115 grams	125 grams
8 ounces (1/2 pound)	225 grams	225 grams
16 ounces (1 pound)	455 grams	500 grams
1 pound	455 grams	0.5 kilogram

MEASUREMENTS

Inches	Centimeters
1	2.5
2	5.0
3	7.5
4	10.0
5	12.5
6	15.0
7	17.5
8	20.5
9	23.0
10	25.5
11	28.0
12	30.5
13	33.0

TEMPERATURES

Fahrenheit	Celsius
32°	0°
212°	100°
250°	120°
275°	140°
300°	150°
325°	160°
350°	180°
375°	190°
400°	200°
425°	220°
450°	230°
475°	240°
500°	260°

NOTE: The recipes in this cookbook have not been developed or tested using metric measures. When converting recipes to metric, some variations in quality may be noted.

Index

Page numbers in *italics* refer to photographs.